FIRST TIME B.....

A CHORAL SINGER'S HANDBOOK

Ian Assersohn

Published in 2008
© 2008 Ian Assersohn.
All rights reserved.
This revision: April 2008

ISBN 978-0-9556949-0-5

Email: iassersohn@btinternet.com
Web: www.lulu.com/content/2126943

Contents

Introduction

The English choral tradition, at least four centuries old, thrives today as one of the country's cultural glories, and one in which just about anyone can participate.

You don't need to be a musician, or even particularly musically literate, to enjoy singing in a choir, and to contribute to the music-making. But the more musical knowledge you have, the more you will enjoy it, and the quicker you will pick up your part.

Singing with others can be a great joy. If you know what you are doing it gets even more fun. This book will, I hope, help you understand the music better, respond more quickly to the intentions of your conductor and generally expand your musical horizons.

The aim of this book is to help you, the enthusiastic but possibly slightly bewildered chorister, to get more out of your choir time, and to pick up a little useful and interesting musical knowledge along the way. I haven't assumed any specialist musical knowledge to being with, so even if you think you know little or nothing about it, this book is for you.

This book is probably best read straight through from front to back, because each item builds on what goes before.

The first part covers basic musical theory. Part two, the main meat of the book, covers basic musical notation. Part three includes some remarks about the business of singing itself and the final part is a very brief introduction to the choral repertoire and the history of music.

As an appendix, there is a handy timeline showing the full name, dates and nationalities of all the composers mentioned in this book.

Before we get started, you ought to know that this book sits firmly in the Western classical music tradition. There are other traditions, other notations, and other stories to be told. But the fact is I'm not the man to tell them, and you won't find them in here.

Acknowledgements

I would like to thank Jan for her insights, advice and patience in helping me prepare this book.

I would also like to thank the members of Leatherhead Choral Society and Barisons Chamber Choir who inspired me to write it. Especially Nik, who gave me the idea.

PART ONE: MUSICAL BASICS

Pulse

The German inventor, engineer and showman Johann Nepomuk Maelzel (1772-1838) is credited with perfecting one of the most useful tools available to the musician; the *metronome*.

Maelzel's metronome, patented in 1815, consists of a small elongated pyramid containing an ingenious clock-work mechanism fronted by a long weighted rod. The clockwork swings the rod at an even rate from side to side making a regular clicking noise, and the speed, or *tempo*, can be varied by sliding the weight up and down. A scale on the front allows the user to set specific number of clicks per minute.

To give you a feel for the scale, sixty beats a minute – one a second - feels like a pretty slow pulse. One hundred and eighty feels like a pretty fast one. If you whistle the "Colonel Bogie" march you're probably going about one hundred and twenty beats a minute.

The use of the metronome in the nineteenth century allowed composers, for the first time, to specify in their scores precisely how fast they wanted their music performed. (Maelzel's friend Ludwig van Beethoven was one of the first to make extensive use of this in his scores). Just as importantly, by setting the metronome going while they were practising, music students could make sure they were keeping to a regular, even tempo.

The metronome makes audible the music's underlying *pulse,* or *beat.* Without it you cannot hear the music's pulse directly, even though as a listener you are always aware of it. The pulse is something that you feel. It's perhaps most obvious in dance music, or marches, but it's always there.

Amateur musicians sometimes it find hard to maintain a strong feeling of the music's pulse continuing unchanged regardless of the speed of the notes. As a singer you may be asked to hold a single note for eight beats, or to sing music with many notes per beat. None of that should affect the beat, or pulse itself, which ticks on regardless.

One of the jobs of a conductor or choirmaster is to transmit a sense of the music's pulse, through gesture, to the performers. One of your jobs, as a singer, is to pick it up.

Sometimes the pulse is meant to vary in a musical performance, and there are various ways of notating this in the score. It is normal practice to slow the pulse at the end of a piece, whether it's written or not, unless the composer explicitly tells you not to.

To help you feel pulse more securely, try this exercise. Sitting down, set up a slowish pulse by tapping one hand on your knee or a table. This hand is the metronome, and must not vary through the exercise.

Now start tapping different note lengths with your other hand, at first slowly and then faster and faster. Begin by tapping once with your right hand for every 4 beats/taps of your left hand. Then switch to every three. Then two. Then one. Now tap twice for every beat, then three times, and finally four times.

When you can do that comfortably, try removing the "metronome" taps but keep them going silently in your head.

Pitch

Some musical notes, or pitches, are "high" and some "low", It's not obvious why we use those words, or why we feel such a strong association between pitch and height, but the association may come directly from the human voice and the experience of singing.

Try this: Hum a low note – the lowest you can reach, and then slowly slide up until you reach the highest note you can. Try to be aware of the music inside you and try to feel where it is in your body. You will, I am sure, feel the low notes located somewhere in your chest and the high notes located towards the top of your head.

This is partly an illusion since the part of you making the noise isn't moving up through your body. But you're making different bits of you resonate, and that's what you're feeling as the movement.

There is also an association between musical pitch and physical size, or weight. Generally speaking big things, if they make sounds at all, make low ones, and small things high ones.

Of course there's only so much you can do musically by just sliding up and down. Most musical systems use the concept of distinct and separate pitches, or notes.

Note names

I'm going to base this section around the keyboard because it's familiar to most people, and is probably the easiest way to envisage musical notes. But everything I am going to say applies equally to any pitched instrument, or to the voice.

Western classical music uses 12 different notes. Seven of the notes, which correspond with the white keys on a piano keyboard, are named using the first seven letters of the alphabet: A, B, C, D, E, F and G. The other five, which correspond with the black keys, are thought of as modifications of these basic seven.

The distance between one note and the next, white or black, is known as a *semitone*. If you move up or down by two semitones you've moved a *tone*.

Notice how, in this picture of part of a piano keyboard, the black keys are grouped into twos and threes. Find a group of three black keys and the key for the note A is just to the right of the second one. Keep moving to the right up the white keys and you'll find the notes B, C, D, E, F and G. The next white key to the right of G is A again. You can see that the pattern of black keys repeats itself, and so do the note names.

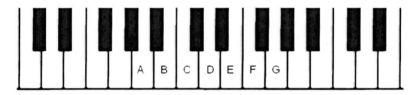

That leaves the five black keys unaccounted for. These represent notes thought of as modifications, raised or lowered versions, of the other seven.

A raised note is said to be *sharpened* and a lowered one is said to be *flattened*. So if you move up a semitone from A, then you get to A *sharp*. If you move down a semitone from A you get to A *flat*.

If you have sharpened or flattened a note and then want to go back to the unvaried white key note, we refer to this as a *natural*.

When any of these three signs occur in a piece of music they are known as *accidentals*. The musical signs for accidentals are:

Sharp   ♯
Flat   ♭
Natural ♮

Now we can fill in the rest of the names of the keys on our piano keyboard. Notice how there are alternative names for the black keys; for example A sharp is also B flat. We'll see later why this is.

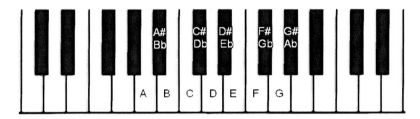

An important thing to be aware of is that there are black keys between *most* of the white keys but not *all* of them. There are no black keys between B and C or between E and F. Another way of saying the same thing is that there are two semitones – a tone – between most white keys. But the distance from B to C is a semitone, and the distance from E to F is also a semitone.

It's not only the black keys that can have multiple names. The note a semitone above B is C, but it is also B sharp. F is also E sharp. It works going the other way too: The note a semitone below C is B, but also C flat. E is also F flat.

Notes that are "spelled" differently but sound the same (like C sharp and D flat) are said to be *enharmonically* equivalent.

You even get *double sharps* and *double flats*, where the notes are raised or lowered by *two* semitones. So for example C sharp is also B double-sharp and E flat is also F double-flat.

Double sharp   𝄪

Double flat   𝄫

There are eight Cs on a full width piano keyboard. The fourth one up, right in the middle of the keyboard is often referred to as "Middle C". This note is around the bottom of the soprano range, and around the top of the bass range.

Middle C is sometimes also referred to as "C4". In the "scientific notation" system, each C is assigned a number, with C1 being near the bottom of the piano and C8 the top.

All other notes take their number from the C immediately below them. So the notes above C4 are D4, E4, F4, G4, A4 and B4. I will use this notation in what follows, where I need to distinguish notes with the same name in different registers.

Rhythm

Rhythm describes the way musical sounds follow one another in time. The rhythm of the music is a changing pattern overlying the steady, unchanging tick of the music's pulse.

In almost all music most of the notes are as fast or faster than the underlying pulse and so the rhythm sub-divides the basic beat into two, three, four or even more sub-beats. Generally the rhythmic stresses fall on the beats and unstressed notes fall between them.

Music in which the pulse is divided into **two,** or multiples of two, is said to be in *simple* time. The nursery rhyme "Mary had a little lamb", for example, is based around a pattern of two notes to the beat, one stressed and one unstressed:

Ma-ry **had** a **litt**-le **lamb,** its **fleece** was **white** as **snow**.

Music in which the pulse is divided into **three,** or multiples of three, is said to be in *compound* time. An example of a tune in compound time is the nursery rhyme "Hickory Dickory Dock". This is based on a pattern of three notes to the beat, one stressed and two unstressed:

Hick-o-ry **Dick**-o-ry **Dock**.

To make things more interesting, music sometimes plays around with the feeling of pulse, placing musical stresses off the beat, i.e. on notes in between the main beats. This effect is known as *syncopation*.

Intervals

The difference in pitch between two notes is called an *interval*. The name of an interval depends on the number of notes spanned. For example, the interval between C and G is called a *fifth* because it spans 5 notes, including the first and last (C, D, E, F, G). Similarly, C to D is a *second*, C to E and *third*, and so on.

The interval between a note and the next highest note with the same name is called an *octave* because it spans 8 notes (e.g. C, D, E, F, G, A, B, C).

When two voices or parts meet on the same note, they are said to be in *unison*. Theoretically speaking, a unison is an interval too, just like the others.

So far I've just talked about the "white key" notes. But introducing sharps and flats into the mix makes no difference to this naming convention; C to G sharp is still a fifth because it spans five letter names. But C to G sharp sounds different from C to G natural so it's clearly a different flavour of fifth.

In fact fourths, fifths and octaves come in three flavours, and thirds, sixths and sevenths in four flavours.

The four flavours of thirds, sixths and sevenths are called: *major, minor, diminished* and *augmented.*

Diminished intervals are the smallest. Minor intervals are a semitone larger than diminished. Major ones are a semitone larger than minor. Augmented intervals are the biggest of all, being a semitone larger than major.

For example, C to E is a major third (4 semitones), C to E flat a minor third (3 semitones), C to E double-flat a diminished third (2 semitones). Finally, C to E sharp (5 semitones) is an augmented third.

Fourths, fifths and octaves are so-called *"perfect"* intervals. They do not have major and minor variants and so only exist in three flavours: perfect, diminished, and augmented. Again, diminished is the smallest, augmented the largest, and perfect is bang in the middle.

For example: C to G is a perfect fifth (7 semitones), C to G flat is a diminished fifth (6 semitones) and C to G sharp is an augmented fifth (8 semitones).

Each interval produces a characteristic effect. For example a major third can sound mellow, a perfect fifth bleak and open, a minor second harsh and discordant. The following table shows some of the intervals :

Semitones	Interval name	Example
0	Perfect unison	C(4) – C(4)
1	Minor second	C – Db
2	Major second	C – D
3	Minor third	C – Eb
4	Major third	C – E
5	Perfect fourth	C – F
6	Augmented fourth	C – F#
7	Perfect fifth	C – G

8	Minor sixth	C – Ab
9	Major sixth	C – A
10	Minor seventh	C – Bb
11	Major seventh	C – B
12	Perfect Octave	C(4) – C(5)

A combination of notes that seems to blend well is called a *consonance*, or a *consonant* interval. A combination that seems discordant is called a *dissonance* or a *dissonant* interval. It's very subjective: the intervals considered consonant or dissonant has changed over time, with different approaches to tuning, and depends very largely on context anyhow.

A lot of people find it helps them to sing intervals if they associate them with tunes that they know well. Here are some examples of tunes and the intervals between the first two (different) notes:

Major 2nd	Happy birthday; God save the Queen
Major 3rd	While shepherds watched their flocks by night
Perfect 4th	Away in a manger
Perfect 5th	Twinkle, twinkle little star
Major 6th	My bonny lies over the ocean
Minor 7th	There's a place for us *from* West Side Story
Perfect 8ve	Over the rainbow *from* The Wizard of Oz

Octaves and unisons are the most consonant intervals in music but the perfect fifth comes close behind. Fifths are important elements in structuring chords, in harmonic progressions and in tuning, as we shall see.

Intervals that are very close to consonances tend to sound very dissonant. A minor second (one semitone, for example C to C sharp) is just a semitone away from being a unison. It sounds very dissonant and "clashy" when the two notes sound together. A major seventh (eleven semitones, for example C to B), is a semitone away from being an octave and also sounds harsh when played together.

But the most notoriously discordant interval of all is the augmented fourth (made up of six semitones, or three whole tones, for example C to F sharp). This interval is one semitone smaller than a perfect fifth, and exactly half of an octave. There's just something wrong sounding about this interval. Its technical name is the *tritone* but in the Middle

Ages it acquired the Latin nickname *diabolus in musica*, the devil in music and was strictly forbidden by music theorists. Most people find it a difficult interval to sing, and a lot of choir members I know would happily go along with the *diabolus* nickname, or worse!

The circle of fifths

I said before that perfect fifths are important intervals in structuring chords, in tuning, and in chord progressions. They also have another interesting property.

If you pile perfect fifths on top of each other, you visit all 12 musical notes before you get back to the one you started with.

For example, if you make your lowest note C and move up a perfect fifth you reach G. Another perfect fifth takes you to D, then A, and so on all the way back to C via all 12 notes.

This can also be drawn in a circle, the so-called *Circle of Fifths*. We will revisit this circle later, in the section on keys where it becomes clear why the fifth is important in chord progressions.

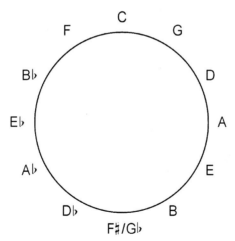

Temperament

First, though, we'll take a short excursion into physics (don't panic) and look at why fifths are important in tuning.

Sound is made up of waves, and the *frequency* of a sound wave is a measurement of the number of waves per second, measured in *Hertz* (after the 19th Century German physicist Heinrich Hertz).

If you adjust a note's frequency up or down a little, without it actually becoming a different note, you are said to be changing its *tuning*. The word *temperament* refers to a complete system of tuning for all the notes. Several different temperaments have been adopted over the centuries, and all of them, it must be said, have advantages and disadvantages.

The temperament in general use today is known as equal temperament, but it's a comparatively recent development and mathematically quite advanced. You may be surprised to learn that it wasn't really possible to tune keyboard instruments accurately using this temperament until the invention of the tuning fork in 1834.

As we have seen, the interval between a note and the next one with the same name is called an *octave*. In terms of sound waves, the upper note has a frequency exactly twice that of the lower, a ratio of 2:1. This make an octave so consonant that the ear perceives the two notes as almost the same.

All western systems of temperament use perfectly tuned octaves but other notes are not so easy to tune.

Mediaeval music used a temperament, a system of tuning, based on fifths and attributed to the Greek philosopher and mathematician Pythagoras. The idea is that you pick a starting point, say C, and tune the interval C-G to be exactly a fifth using the simplest possible ratio, 3:2. Then you use your top note as a new starting point and tune another fifth (G-D) then another and so on. As we've seen, if you keep going like this you eventually get back to C, having visited, and tuned, all 12 notes.

So if you tune the note A4 to a frequency of 440 Hertz, the modern convention, then using Pythagorean tuning you should tune E5 to 660 Hertz. This will give you a beautiful sounding fifth, with no distracting "beating" effect.

Once you have E5 you can find E4, E6 and all the other Es by dividing or multiplying by two. Then you find B, again using 660 as your new starting point and the same ratio of 3:2, which gives you 990. And so on through all twelve notes.

Unfortunately, though, when you get all the way round the circle and back to A, you will find you aren't where you meant to be. You should end up with A5 at 880 Hertz, twice the frequency of the note you started with. But in fact A5 will be around 892 Hertz, a teeny bit high. Even worse, although your fifths will sound great, some of the other intervals will sound distinctly off colour, with the unpleasant "beating" effect characteristic of slightly-out-of-tune intervals.

Clearly another solution had to be found. Various other temperaments have been suggested over time, each with their own advantages and disadvantages. There is no perfect answer, unfortunately.

In our current equal temperament system the ratio between adjacent semitones is always the same (it's the twelfth root of two, if you're interested). So if A is 440 Hz, E comes out around 659 Hz, slightly flatter than the Pythagorean "ideal" of 660 but very close.

For singers, this is more than just theoretical stuff. Sixteenth century madrigals, for example, were written with a specific temperament in mind, and they just don't sound the same when sung with equal temperament. Some intervals that sound dissonant in equal temperament would have sounded consonant then, and vice versa.

So if anyone tells you you're singing out of tune, try telling them you're simply experimenting with a different temperament. That should shut them up.

Keys and scales

Pretty much all Western music written before the 20th Century, does not use all twelve notes equally. Instead, at any one time it uses a relatively small set of notes, sometimes as few as five, but most often seven. The set of notes being used is called the *mode*. Different modes have different characteristics and are associated with different moods.

In most modes one of the notes feels like "home", a note on which the music can rest. Other notes feel like they are being pulled by a sort of gravitational attraction towards that home note. The home note is special. Tunes often start, and almost always end on it.

In music theory this special home note is called the *key note* or *tonic*. Any of the twelve semitones in an octave can be the tonic, but to make it sound correctly like a tonic, the other notes have to be chosen correctly to build the mode around it.

Historically, Western Music has used many modes but most music written between the seventeenth and twentieth centuries, and much of it written since, uses just two. These are known as the *Major* and *Minor* modes and each one uses seven notes.

Pieces written using the major mode are often characterised as sounding "happy" and those using the minor mode as sounding "sad". This is too broad a generalisation but it has a grain of truth in it.

There are actually two variants of the minor mode called *Melodic* and *Harmonic* minor, but we'll come to that.

If you string out the seven notes of a mode in order you get a *scale*.

All the notes of the scale, not just the tonic, have special technical names. The next table shows you what they are.

Position	Technical name	Example in C Major
1	Tonic	C
2	Supertonic	D
3	Mediant	E
4	Subdominant	F
5	Dominant	G
6	Submediant	A
7	Leading note	B

It's easier to see the sense of some of these names if you don't think of the tonic as being at the bottom of a scale but as being in the middle of a span of notes.

The dominant is a fifth above the tonic, the *sub*dominant is a fifth below.

The mediant is a third above the tonic, the *sub*mediant a third below.

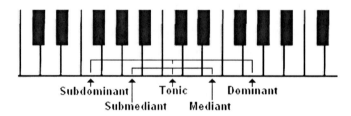

The leading note is so-called because it gives a strong feeling of leading up to the tonic.

Supertonic is just a boring name for the note above the tonic.

Major scales

To construct a major scale, you pick a note to be the tonic and then count up the right number of semitones to get to each note following this pattern:

Tone - tone - semitone - tone - tone - tone - semitone

Yet another way to think of it is as two symmetrical half-scales each made up of two tones and a semitone, the first starting on the tonic and the second on the fifth note of the scale, the dominant. These four-note mini-scales are known as tetrachords, which I wanted to tell you because I love the word, but you really don't need to remember it.

You can create a major scale using just the seven "white key" notes A to G, with no need for sharps or flats. To do this you start on C.

This is one reason for the apparently odd layout of black and white keys on the piano keyboard: it makes it easy to play in C major.

You can construct a major scale on any of the twelve notes, but all of them apart from C major will involve the use of "black key" notes.

Minor scales

The minor mode goes:

Tone - semitone - tone - tone - semitone - tone - tone

You can also play a minor scale on the white keys, this time by starting on A

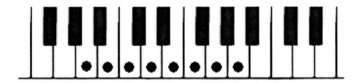

There is a problem with the minor mode, which is the tone between the seventh (leading) note and the tonic. Some important harmonic progressions don't work well unless the leading note is a semitone below the tonic. So the basic minor scale as described above is hardly used in actual music, but varied in one of two ways.

One way is called the *Harmonic Minor* scale. This works by simply sharpening the leading note to create a semitone between it and the tonic. So to create a harmonic minor scale starting on A you use a G sharp, instead of a G natural.

The pattern is now

Tone - semitone - tone - tone - semitone - tone-&-a-half - semitone

This solves the harmony problem, but it causes others. By raising the seventh note, to make it closer to the tonic, it has got further away from the sixth note, making that awkward tone-and-a-half (augmented second) interval (for example F to G#).

This gives tunes (melodies) written using the harmonic minor scale an awkward gap to get round. The second type of minor scale, the *Melodic minor* scale, deals with this by sharpening the sixth note too.

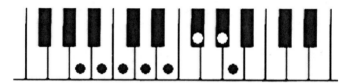

That partially solves the problem. Unfortunately this only sounds good on the way *up*. On the way *down*, it just doesn't seem to work so well. So the melodic minor scale, uniquely, is different on the way down from the way up. Going down it flattens both the sixth and seventh notes again and reverts to the original theoretical minor scale we started with in the first place!

Keys

As we have seen, the major scale starting on C (C Major) is the only major scale you can play entirely on the white keys; i.e. the only scale which needs no flats or sharps. Other scales need to use the black keys to keep the pattern of tones and semitones consistent.

Remember I said that the dominant note of a scale is a perfect fifth above the tonic, and the subdominant is a perfect fifth below? This knowledge can help you to find out how many "black key" notes are needed in each scale.

We start from C major, the scale with no "black key" notes; no sharps or flats.

The major key with one sharp is built on the dominant of C, namely G major.

The major key with two sharps is built on the dominant of G, namely D major.

See the pattern? To find the key with one extra sharp, you go up a perfect fifth, to the dominant note of the key you started with.

The new sharp added to each key is always the seventh note (the leading note) of the scale. For example, in G major the added sharp is F sharp.

Because the new sharp is always the same note of the scale, the pattern of sharps is also based on fifths: F, C, G, D, A.

This table shows the pattern for the first six sharps.

Major key	Number of sharps	Sharps
C	0	
G	1	F
D	2	F, C
A	3	F, C, G
E	4	F, C, G, D
B	5	F, C, G, D, A
F sharp	6	F, C, G, D, A, E

Now for the flat keys. The major key with one flat is built on the *sub*dominant of C, namely F major.

The major key with two flats is built on the *sub*dominant of F, namely B flat.

The pattern here is in a sense the opposite of the first one. To find the key with one extra flat, you go *down* a perfect fifth to the subdominant note of the key you started with. That's equivalent to going up a perfect fourth.

The new flat added to each key is always the fourth note of the scale. For example, in F major the added flat is B flat.

Because the new flat is always the same note of the scale, the pattern of flats is also based on perfect fourths: B, E, A, D, G.

This table shows the pattern for the first six flats.

Major key	Number of flats	Flats
C	0	
F	1	B
B flat	2	B, E
E flat	3	B, E, A
A flat	4	B, E, A, D
D flat	5	B, E, A, D, G
G flat	6	B, E, A, D, G, C

The circle of fifths gives us a neat way of showing this pattern. The circle shows the number of sharps or flats needed for the major scale starting on each note – increasing numbers of sharps as you move clockwise round the circle and flats as you move anticlockwise.

Going clockwise around the circle - the sharp direction - takes you through a pattern of rising fifths, and going anticlockwise - the flat direction - through a pattern of falling fifths.

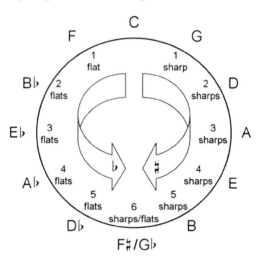

So far we've only dealt with major keys but there is also a circle of fifths for the minor keys.

For every major key there is an equivalent minor key with the same number of sharps or flats. This is known as the *relative minor* key.

The relative minor is always the key starting on its relative major's submediant (the sixth note of the scale). Another way to think of this is to count three semitones down from the relative major's tonic.

For example, the relative minor of C major is A minor.

Another way to find the relative minor is to count three steps round the circle of fifths. The next diagram shows the circle with arrows joining each major key to its relative minor.

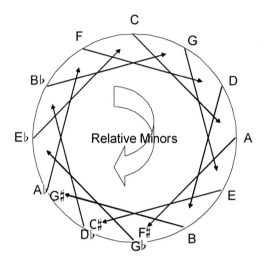

To find the relative major of each minor key, simply reverse the direction of the arrows.

Chords

A set of more than two notes sounding together is called a *chord*. A very common type of chord is made by taking three alternate notes of a scale. For example, in C Major you could choose C, E and G, or perhaps F, A and C. This type of chord is called a *triad*.

When the bottom note, also called the *root* of the chord, is the keynote, or tonic, then the chord is a *tonic triad*.

Tonic triads are used all the time. It's a very good idea for a singer to get good at finding the notes of a tonic triad given one of the other notes.

Tonic triads in *major* keys are made up of a major third with a minor third on top, for example C, E, G. This type of triad, not surprisingly, is called a major triad.

Tonic triads in *minor* keys are made up or a minor third with a major third on top, for example C, E flat, G. This is a minor triad.

The top note of the triad is the same in both cases; it's only the middle note, the mediant, that changes between major and minor tonic triads.

You can make triads on any note of the scale, not just the tonic. The second most common triad, after the tonic, is on the dominant. Unlike the tonic triad, the dominant triad is always major, regardless of whether it occurs in a major key or a minor key. For example, in either C major or C minor the dominant triad would be G, B, D.

Triads on other notes of the scale are sometimes major, sometimes minor. You also find augmented triads (two major thirds on top of each other) and diminished triads (two minor thirds on top of each other).

Modulations and chromatic notes

So far I've been talking as if all music only uses the seven notes of the chosen key. That's been a useful simplification to get us started but I have to admit it's not strictly true. In fact it's not even remotely true, for two reasons.

Firstly, music seldom stays in one key for very long. Most music of any length moves through one or more additional keys as a way of creating contrast and a feeling of progression, of going on a journey. The process of moving from one key to another is known as *modulation*.

The closer two keys are to each other in the circle of fifths, the easier it is to modulate from one to the other, because it involves the fewest note changes. Most modulations are to the dominant or subdominant key. The other common modulation is to the relative minor or relative major.

For example, in C major, adding an F sharp creates a modulation to G major and adding a B flat creates one to F major. Actually it's not quite a simple as that, because it has to be done in the right way for it to sound smooth and natural, but you get the idea.

Classical movements always begin and end in the same key, regardless of how often they modulate in the middle. A fresh outcrop of accidentals in the middle of a piece may suggest that a modulation has taken place.

Another use of accidentals is to provide a little extra "colour" to the music without actually changing key. The seven official notes of the scale, known as *diatonic* notes, can sometimes be joined by other notes from outside the key, not in this case as part of a modulation but as a kind of musical 'seasoning'.

These notes visiting from outside the key are known as *chromatic* notes (from the Greek word for colour, chroma). The use and abuse of chromatic notes varies between different musical styles and periods, but in general reached something of a frenzied peak in the heavy romanticism of the late nineteenth century.

And with that, it's time to move on to part two and talk about how music is represented on the printed page, and how to interpret the various symbols and text that you will come across in vocal scores.

In other words, we're going to talk about musical notation.

PART TWO: MUSICAL NOTATION

The notation used for Western music has evolved over many centuries into a representational system of extraordinary richness and subtlety. It attempts an essentially impossible task: to represent on the printed page any sounds, shapes, emotions and patterns which can be made in music. That it so nearly achieves this ambition is truly wonderful.

In terms of the amount of information conveyed, musical notation far exceeds most graphical representations. A tiny fragment of musical manuscript can indicate duration, pitch, volume, attack, tone and dynamic variation in such a compressed and unambiguous manner that a trained and experienced musician can take it all in at a glance and seemingly effortlessly and instantaneously reproduce the sound on their instrument or with their voice.

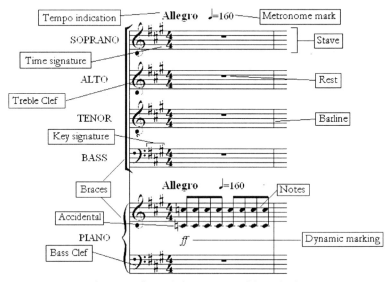

Anatomy of a musical score: some of the main elements

Many musical instructions take the form of symbols which take up little space on the page and need no translation to be understood by musicians from any country. But there are still many other directions which require words or phrases in plain text. This potentially introduces language problems for performers, so quite early on musicians adopted Italian as a common language, reflecting the predominance of Italian music at the time, and there are many Italian terms still in common use. I will introduce the more common ones as we go through.

The basic idea of musical notation is that the horizontal dimension on the page represents time and the vertical dimension represents pitch.

Music flows from left to right across the page on a series of 5-lined grids called *staves*. Each stave represents one, two or sometimes even more, lines of music so as a singer you might find yourself sharing a stave with another voice part.

The musical texture at any moment may be made up of several voice and instrumental parts singing and playing at the same time, involving the use of several staves. The group of staves that represent all the music happening at a particular moment is called a *system*. Systems are joined together with braces - sometimes curly, sometimes straight, at the beginning of each line.

The notes themselves are represented as little circles, or ovals, sometimes with 'sticks', or stems attached. The shape of these stemmed or un-stemmed ovals represents the duration of the notes.

It's important to understand that the shape of a note tells you nothing about when to *begin* it, just how long to hold it for once it has begun.

Note durations

The longest lasting note you're ever likely to meet is called a *breve*. The name breve derives from the Latin for "brief", by way of a mediaeval note called a *brevis*. How this came to stand for a rather long note is a long story which I won't bore you with right now. Breves are rare in most music so I include it here mainly for completeness. There are a few different ways of drawing breves, but these two are most common.

The longest note in common use today is the *semibreve*, which lasts for half as long as a breve. They are also called, more pragmatically but less poetically, *whole notes*. This makes breves, somewhat ridiculously, *double whole notes*. Semibreves look like breves without the 'whiskers'.

A *minim, (half note)* is half as long as a semibreve. You make a minim by adding a *stem* to a semibreve. Stems can point either up or down - there are rules about this which we'll talk about later.

A *Crotchet* (*quarter note*), pronounced "Croh-tchet" is half as long as a minim. You make a crotchet by shading in the head of a minim.

A *quaver* (*eighth note*) is half as long as a crotchet. You make a quaver by adding a *tail,* (or *flag*) to a crotchet's stem.

When quavers directly follow one another, their tails can join up to make *beams*, so that they look like this.

There used to be a convention in vocal music (more honoured in the breach than the observance) for tails to be kept separate when sung to different syllables. You will still see this in older editions but thankfully most contemporary editions use conventional beaming rules for vocal music.

Once you get shorter durations than quavers, the naming convention changes and everything is a variant on 'quaver'. Thus we have the *semiquaver* (*sixteenth* note), the *demisemiquaver* (*thirty-second* note), and the *hemidemisemiquaver* (*sixty-fourth* note). You make all these notes by adding more and more tails or beams to the stem. For example, semiquavers look like this.

And demisemiquavers look like this.

So to recapitulate, taking the semibreve, or whole note, as the standard unit, and successively dividing in half you can fit two minims, four crotchets, eight quavers or sixteen semiquavers in to the same length of time as one semibreve.

You can make up any other note lengths you want by joining these basic building blocks together using a curved line, known as a *tie*. For example, if you tie a crotchet to a quaver – a quarter note to an eighth note - you get a note that's 3/8 of a semibreve long. If you tie a minim to a crotchet – a half note to a quarter note - you get a note that's ¾ of a semibreve long. This picture shows a crotchet tied to a quaver:

This sort of thing is so common that a musical notation shorthand has developed. Here a simple dot is added immediately following a note to indicate that the note should be held for half as long again as normal. The note becomes a *dotted note*. So a dotted minim is the same as a minim tied to a crotchet. You can dot any note length in this way.

The dotted crotchet on the left of this picture last exactly as long as the crotchet tied to a quaver on the right:

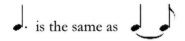

You also find *double dots*. The first dot adds a half and the second dot adds another *quarter* to the basic note length. So a double-dotted crotchet is equivalent to a crotchet tied to a quaver tied to a semiquaver – a quarter plus an eighth plus a sixteenth:

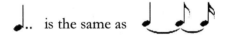

The next diagram summarises the most common basic note durations in order, with the longest at the top. Each line takes up the same amount of time.

Rests

For every note length there is an equivalent *rest*. A rest is simply an interval of time between notes. The musical pulse carries right on through rests, which make them as important to the music as the notes.

This table shows the main note lengths and their equivalent rests.

Breve		
Semibreve		
Minim		
Crotchet		
Quaver		
Semiquaver		
Demisemiquaver		

Breve, semibreve and minim rests all look very similar, so notice that breve rests fill the space between two stave lines (we'll talk about staves later), semibreve rests hang down below a line, and minim rests (being shorter and "lighter" than semibreves) sit on top of a line.

People often remember the shape of a crotchet rests as looking like a child's drawing of a seagull turned sideways.

Quaver rests are like little number "7"s. Similarly to the way extra tails are added to quavers to make shorter notes, rests shorter than quavers are made by adding extra stripes to the "7": two stripes for semiquavers, three for demisemiquavers and so on.

You can also add dots and double dots after rests to make them longer, just as you can with notes.

A dotted crotchet rest, for example, lasts the same length of time as a dotted crotchet note, i.e. three quavers.

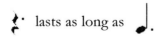

A dotted quaver rest, for example, lasts the same length of time as a dotted quaver note, i.e. Three semiquavers.

 lasts as long as 𝅘𝅥𝅮.

In some French editions and in the older Novello editions you still find knocking about, you may also see crotchet rests written as back-to-front quaver rests:

These are very confusing to read. I really don't know what these editors were thinking, and I would like to apologise to you on their behalf for any mistakes they may cause you to make.

Dotted note patterns

Some rhythmical patterns are very common. One of these is made up by a dotted crotchet followed by quaver. Because a dotted crotchet is worth, as you know, three quavers, this pattern takes up four quavers, a minim.

𝅘𝅥. 𝅘𝅥𝅮 lasts as long as 𝅗𝅥

The same principle applies, at a smaller scale to a dotted quaver followed by a semiquaver,

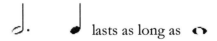

and at a larger scale to a dotted minim followed by a crotchet.

𝅗𝅥. 𝅘𝅥 lasts as long as 𝅝

Relating durations to the beat

The underlying beat of the music can be attached to pretty much any note length. You may have been taught at some point in your musical education that a crotchet is "one beat". That's often true, but certainly not always. To explain this further, we need to talk about bar lines and time signatures.

Bar lines and time signatures

As we've seen, the musical pulse flows along, indicated by regular beats. However not all beats are equally important. Because of the way the rhythm and melody are laid out, some beats (like some people) receive more *stress*.

Pretty well all music written between the seventeenth and twentieth centuries, and much of it since, has regular stresses that fall, usually, every two, three or four beats.

Beats are divided into these regular groups by *bar lines* (or *barlines*); vertical lines written from top to bottom of each stave in the score.

The distance between each bar line is known, simply, as a *bar* and the major stress in each bar normally falls on the first beat after each bar line, in other words the first beat of the bar. In this famous example from Handel's *Messiah*, the word "Hallelujah" receives stresses successively on the first, third and second syllables, as shown.

The end of a section is shown by a *double bar* - literally two barlines next to each other, as in this extract from *Timor et tremor* by Lasso

And the end of the piece is shown by a special double bar with one thin and one thick line. This is the end of *Cantique de Jean Racine* by Fauré

Time signatures are written as pairs of numbers, one over the other. They look a bit like fractions and you will find one at the start of every piece.

Time signatures are read top to bottom; for example "three four".

$$\frac{3}{4}$$

In time signatures representing simple time the top number indicates the number of beats in a bar, the bottom number the note length that makes up the beat.

Time signatures are vital pieces of information because they indicate both the length of a beat and number of beats in a bar.

To understand time signatures, and bar lines, it helps to relate them back to the familiar rhythms and stresses of poetry, or rather verse.

> Oh the grand old duke of York,
>
> He had ten thousand men.
>
> He marched them up to the top of the hill
>
> And he marched them down again.

If you recite this rhyme you will find yourself automatically stressing certain syllables more than others. 'Grand', 'York', 'had', and 'men' are stressed whereas 'Oh', 'the', 'old', 'duke' etc are not.

One thing to notice is that the first stressed syllable is not at the start of the first line. That's because the first line starts on what musicians call an *upbeat* or *anacrusis*; an unstressed syllable, or group of syllables which lead you towards the first proper stress, the *downbeat*.

Here is the verse again, with a "bar line" before each major stress:

> Oh the | *grand* old duke of | *York*,
>
> He | *had* ten thousand | *men*.
>
> *He* | *marched* them up to the | *top* of the hill
>
> And he | *marched* them down a- | *gain*.

As in music, the stresses in the verse occur as the first "beats" in each "bar".

I said before that 'duke' was unstressed, but that's oversimplifying. 'duke' is less stressed than 'grand' but more stressed than 'old'. That's because 'duke' falls on a beat, the second beat of the bar, and 'old' falls in between the beats.

So musically speaking this verse has two beats in every bar, and each of those beats has a tick in the middle – e.g. 'old' and 'of'. If this verse was written with a time signature, then, it could well be 2/4, meaning two crotchet (quarter note) beats in the bar.

One of the easiest ways of killing a musical performance stone dead is to ignore the musical stresses and sing or play every note in the bar as if it were similarly stressed. Unless they want you to stress an unexpected note composers do not usually indicate where the stresses occur : it's for the performer to interpret.

But back to time signatures. As we've seen, the grand old duke marches along in 2/4 time, what musicians refer to as *duple time*. But of course you can have more than two beats in a bar. For example, you can have *triple time* with three beats in a bar, and *quadruple time* with four.

An example of triple time would be 3/4, three crotchet beats in a bar – the characteristic Oom-pah-pah Oom-pah-pah time of a waltz.

An example of quadruple time would be 4/4, four crotchet beats in a bar. Think of Land of Hope and Glory for an instant idea of what 4/4 sounds like.

In early notation time signatures were often expressed as symbols rather than numbers. Most of these symbols have disappeared but two have survived. The *common time* symbol shown here means exactly the same as 4/4.

$$\mathfrak{C}$$

Although the symbol looks like a letter C, contrary to popular belief it was not originally a C standing for "common time" but a broken circle indicating "imperfect" time as opposed to triple time, which was represented by a complete circle. Triple time was considered "perfect", because of the importance of the number 3 in mediaeval times, and its links with the Holy Trinity.

The *alla breve* symbol, sometimes called *cut common time* shown here means the same as 2/2: two minim beats in a bar:

$$\mathfrak{C}\!\!\!|\cdot$$

One other rule about time signatures: every bar must have the correct number of beats in it with the exception of the first and last bars. If the piece begins on an anacrusis (upbeat) then the first bar will not contain a full complement of beats; you have to figure out which beat of the bar you are starting on. In this example, the opening of *My love dwelt in a northern land* by Elgar, the rhythm begins on the third and last beat of the bar.

But, by convention, the first and last bars of a piece must add up to a complete bar. This means that if the piece does begin on an anacrusis, then the value of the anacrusis has to be taken off the last bar of the piece. Here is the end of the same piece. Notice how the last bar only has two beats.

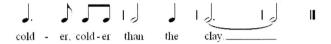

cold - er, cold-er   than   the   clay._____

Practical exercises

At this point I thought it would be useful to include some practical rhythmic exercises.

For each rhythm, I suggest you either use a metronome if available or else set up a crotchet pulse by tapping your finger or hand on a table or your knee. I'll indicate the beat with little arrowheads, like this:

    ▲   ▲   ▲   ▲   ▲   ▲   ▲   ▲

These arrowhead are not real musical notation; we're just using them for now to help show you where the beats are.

After you set up the beat, you start singing the rhythm. We're going to use very specific nonsense syllables. It doesn't matter which pitch you choose – just pick one you like!

Every time you sing a note on a beat, you say 'Ta'. One of the important things about this system is that you make a new sound on every beat other than rests. Anytime you want to indicate a beat without a new note starting on it, you knock off the consonant. So "Ta" becomes "a".

Ta   ta   a   ta   ta   a   a   a
▲   ▲   ▲   ▲   ▲   ▲   ▲   ▲

When you see a rest, the traditional thing is to sniff. If you find that indelicate then just *think* the rest.

Ta   a   (sniff)   ta   ta   (sniff)   ta   a
▲   ▲   ▲   ▲   ▲   ▲   ▲   ▲

Quavers in between the beats are 'te'. So a pair of quavers is "ta-te":

And finally, semiquavers in between the quavers are 'fe'. So four semiquavers in a beat would go "Ta-fe-te-fe".

Notice how I had to stretch the beats wider apart on the page as I added smaller note values because I wanted to keep the examples in proportion, with the beats evenly spaced. Actual music notation is non-proportional, that is to say the amount of horizontal space between notes on the printed page does not tell you how long the notes last relative to other notes. Only the shape of the note matters in this respect.

The above example re-written using standard non-proportional notation looks more like the following. It's important to realize that it should sound exactly the same as the example above.

Here is a rhythmic exercise with dotted notes.

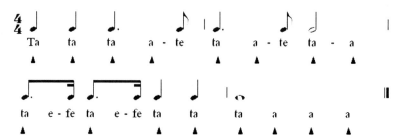

This next example includes some ties. Remember that ties, indicated by the curved lines joining certain notes, create a new note length – you should hold on to the note for the full length of the notes joined by the tie. In this example, the first two ties create note lengths equivalent to a crotchet plus a quaver – three quavers. This could have been written as a dotted crotchet except for the fact that it would have overflowed the bar, creating a bar four and a half beats long.

The rhythm is taken from the *Domine Jesu* in Mozart's *Requiem*.

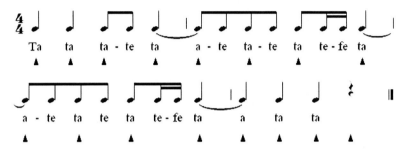

And here is the same example with the original words. Notice how Mozart stretches some syllables over more than one note, a technique known as *melisma*.

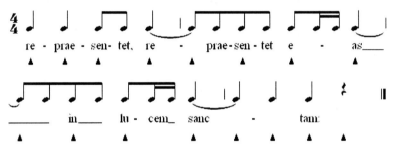

This sort of rhythm, which is an example of syncopation, is quite hard to sing in time, because there is no new note on the first beat of the bar to help fix the pulse. It's very important to feel the stress of the beat at the beginning of the bar still driving the rhythm along.

Syncopation is defined as a displacement of the beat or the normal stress of the music. It is perhaps most closely associated today with jazz styles, but composers of every period have used this device to a greater or lesser extent.

Here is a slightly longer exercise, including dotted notes and rests. This rhythm is from *Lift up your heads, O ye gates* in Handel's *Messiah*.

Now try it with the original words. Keep up the tapping to make sure the rests are the right length, and refer back to the "ta" names to help you with the dotted rhythms. Make sure you can distinguish between the dotted quaver rhythm in "everlasting" and the even quavers in "glory shall come".

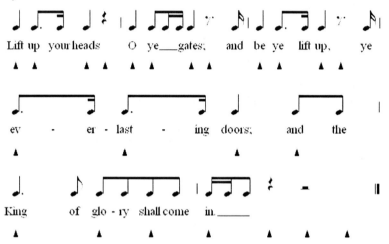

Compound time

All the time signatures I've talked about so far have something in common; the beat can be divided into two sub-beats. One crotchet can be divided into two quavers (one quarter into two eighth notes). As we saw earlier, this is known as *simple* time.

The opposite of simple time, as you may remember, is *compound* time. In compound time the basic beat is a dotted note, which can be divided into three sub-beats instead of the two sub-beats of simple time.

This gives rise to a different sort of rhythmic feel. Instead of a "Tick-tock, tick-tock" feel you get a sort of "tickety tockety, tickety tockety". Earlier I suggested the nursery rhyme "Hickory Dickory Dock" as a well-known example.

As with simple time, compound time comes in duple, triple and quadruple varieties. But unlike simple time, there is a difficulty about how to express compound time in the time signature.

The bottom number of a time signature, as I said earlier, tells the performer what note length represents a beat. In the case of simple time it tells you directly: Four means crotchets because there are four crotchets in a semibreve. Two means minims because there are two minims in a semibreve, and so on.

But dotted notes, which form the beat in compound time, don't fit exactly into a semibreve. There are 2 ½ dotted crotchets in a semibreve.

The way we get round this is to use the sub-beats as the lower note of the time signature in compound time.

If the beat is a dotted crotchet, sub-beats are quavers, three of them per beat. If there are two dotted crotchet beats in the bar, then there are six quavers in a bar. So this would be represented by the time signature 6/8.

6/8 is an example of compound duple time; two dotted crotchet beats in the bar.

Similarly, in compound triple time the top number will be 9 (e.g. 9/8), and in compound quadruple (e.g. 12/8).

Here is another exercise from Mozart's *Requiem*, this time from the opening of the *Lacrimosa*. This example is in 12/8 so there are four dotted crotchet beats in the bar. Remember, each beat has three quavers in it. If you are using the "Ta" names from my previous exercises then you can use the syllables "ta-cka-ty" for these three quavers.

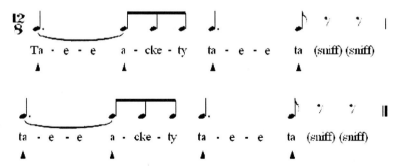

Here is the same example with the original text..

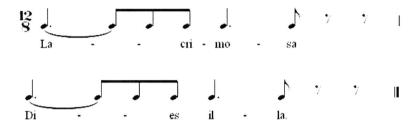

Beyond quadruple time

What happens when you have more than four beats in a bar? The answer might surprise you. When you get to five, e.g. 5/8, the feel of the music jumps back to two-in-a-bar.

Try saying the following rhythm, making sure you leave no gaps between the bars:

Buck-ing-ham Pal-ace | **Buck**-ing-ham Pal-ace | **Buck**-ing-ham Pal-ace |

There are five syllables in the pattern but the musical feel is completely two in a bar, with the beats falling on 'Buck' and 'Pal'. But the beats are not the same length; the first has three syllables (sub-beats) and the second two. It's like walking with one leg longer than other.

So if you see a time signature where the top number is five, be prepared for this slightly disorientating 3+2 (or sometimes 2+3) feel. This example is from the *Gloria* in Rutter's *Mass of the Children*.

And again, with the original words

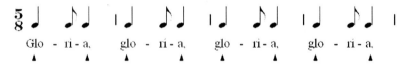

Just as five is a form of duple time with, seven (e.g. 7/8) is a form of triple time. In this case the most common division is 2+2+3, but the other combinations of 3+2+2 and, at a pinch, 2+3+2 are also possible.

It's not quite so easy to come up with a piece of doggerel to illustrate seven. The best I can do is:

Give three cheers for Jim and he'll | **Give** three cheers for Bob and he'll |
Give three cheers ...

This has a 2+2+3 feel; the mini-stresses fall on 'Give', 'cheers' and the name.

There's a real-life example of 7/8 in Britten's *Rejoice in the Lamb,* which also has a 2+2+3 feel.

Ta - e   ta - e   ta -cka - ty   ta - e   ta - e - a - e (sniff)

And with the original words

Nim - rod,   the might - y   hun - ter,_____

Summary of time signatures

This table shows examples of simple and compound duple, triple and quadruple time signatures, along with a bar's worth of beats.

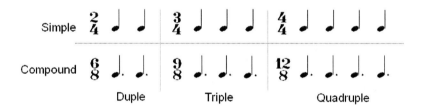

	Duple	Triple	Quadruple
Simple	2/4 ♩ ♩	3/4 ♩ ♩ ♩	4/4 ♩ ♩ ♩ ♩
Compound	6/8 ♩. ♩.	9/8 ♩. ♩. ♩.	12/8 ♩. ♩. ♩. ♩.

Changes of time signature

There's no great mystery about changing time signatures in the middle of a piece: it happens a lot, especially from the second half of the twentieth century onwards.

Sixteenth century music was written for the most part without bar lines so where modern editors have inserted them in an attempt to be helpful you may also see frequent changes of time signature in the music of composers from this period.

One particular type of change merits a comment, though. When the music changes from a simple to a compound time signature, or vice versa, you need to know what relationship the composer intends between the old and the new beats.

For example, say you are moving from a section in 4/4 to one in 6/8. You have to know: does the *beat* stay the same (in which case quavers speed up)? Or do *quavers* stay the same (in which case the beat slows down)?

If you think about it you'll see that it has to be one or the other. Let me say it a different way: If the new beat, which has three quavers in it, stays the same speed as the old beat, which only has two, then quavers now must be going faster than they used to.

On the other hand, if quavers stay the same speed then the beat now takes longer than it used to because there are more quavers in a beat.

Usually the composer will make their intentions clear by specifying how the new time signature relates to the old one. For example, if you see

$$\quarternote = \dottedquarternote$$

this means that the beat stays the same, because the old beat (crotchets) equals the new beat (dotted crotchets).

Similarly if you see

$$\eighthnote = \eighthnote$$

then you know quavers stay the same and the beat speeds up.

If the composer hasn't specified, then you can usually assume the first one, where the beat stays the same.

Tuplets

I'm afraid that when I listed the different note lengths I was holding out on you. There's a whole class of note lengths we haven't talked about yet, called *tuplets*. Tuplets temporarily change the rhythmical feel of the music. Tuplets are marked with a small number above or below the note depending on whether the stems point up or down.

As we've seen, in simple time, beats are divided into two equal parts, and in compound time they are divided into three equal parts. Tuplets are a way of temporarily changing that.

The most common type of tuplet, found in simple time, is the *triplet*. Triplets take beats that normally divide into two and divide them into three. In other words, instead of the two normal subdivisons you get three rather faster ones: it's like a moment of compound time in the midst of simple time.

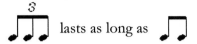

Minims can be divided into three triplet crotchets

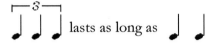

In compound time, where the beat is normally divided into three anyhow, you may find *Duplets*, which are like a little moment of simple time.

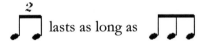

Many other subdivisions are possible, but it's usually fairly obvious what's required once you understand the concept - even if it's not always easy to do in practice.

In this example in simple time, each crotchet beat is divided into one, two, three, four, five and then six equal parts. The subdivisions into one, two and four can be done using normal notes, but the three, five and six need tuplets.

In this example in compound time, each dotted crotchet beat is also divided into one, two, three, four and then six equal parts. This time the subdivisions into one, three and six can be done using normal notes, but the two and four need tuplets.

Here are a couple of exercises to help you get the hang of tuplets.

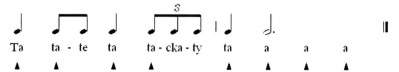

Let's take a closer look at the triplet in the middle of the exercise. If we add little white arrowheads to show where the sub-beats come, you can see that the second and third notes of the triplet don't exactly line up with them.

Try this part of the rhythm using your left hand to tap out the beats and your right hand tapping out the half-beats.

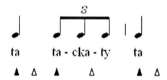

A very common mistake made by amateur singers is to transform this into a combination of semiquavers and quavers that synchronises with the half beat. Try these two similar rhythms and see if you can feel the subtle but important difference between these and the real triplet.

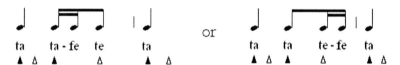

Whole bar rests

I need to say one last thing on rhythm notation, and it's to do with rests. There is one exception to the rest notation I described earlier: By convention, a semibreve rest can also be used to indicate a whole bar's rest regardless of how many beats there are in a bar.

That's the end of the section about the way *rhythm* is written. The next part of the book deals with the notation of musical *pitch*.

Staves

Musical pitches are written on a 5-line grid, called a *stave* (or *staff*).

On the stave, each line, and each space between lines, corresponds to one of the "white key" notes, A to G. So in the following picture we see two next-door "white key" notes.

This picture shows two notes an octave apart.

If I fill in the in-between notes it should make it easier to see the eight notes that make up the octave:

The range of notes you can fit on a stave is about an octave plus a fourth. Remembering that early written music was almost exclusively vocal, it is not really a coincidence that the stave nicely accommodates the range of most singers.

You can extend the range of a stave by temporarily adding mini-lines, called *leger lines* (or *ledger lines*). These can make the music harder to read though, so composers and publishers try to minimise their use. The following example shows an octave extending below the stave using first one and then two leger lines.

Clefs

Different instruments and voices have different ranges. But whatever their range, we want to keep as many notes as possible on the stave, minimising the use of those confusing leger lines.

To cope with this demand, we can define the range of the stave any way we want. Let me explain what I mean. Because the stave can just about accommodate the range of a given voice, if we define the bottom of the stave to be around the bottom note of the specific voice we have in mind, we should have to use very few leger lines (at least for singers).

For example, sopranos don't tend to go below C4 ("middle C") or above A5. This is a range of an octave plus a sixth. If we define the range of the stave as occupying the middle of this range we only need use one leger line at the top of the stave and one at the bottom. For sopranos, anyhow.

And that's exactly how things are organised. The note on the first leger line below the stave is defined as C4. This puts A5 on the first leger line above the stave.

This definition is indicated by the use of a squiggly sign at the start of every line of music.

This symbol, called the *treble clef* or soprano clef, is said to be derived from an elaborate letter 'g'. In any case it establishes the note G4 as being the second line up from the bottom of the stave – the swirl in the centre sort of points to this line. For this reason the treble clef is also sometimes called the G-clef.

With the clef in place we can, at last, write in the note name under the notes.

Many people like to use mnemonics to help them remember the names of the notes on the stave. For the treble stave the notes in the spaces are (from bottom to top)

F - A - C - E

which is about as easy to remember as it could be. No such luck with the treble clef lines, though, which are

E - G - B - D - F

The best known acronym for this is Every Good Boy Deserves Fun. Alternatively, I once held a competition amongst my young students for the best new mnemonic for this and the winning entry was "Eggs Go Bad Decidedly Fast". That was over 20 years ago so I guess it worked for me but if you don't like either of those, feel free to choose another.

Obviously the bass voice is considerably lower than the soprano voice, almost two octaves lower. If we used the same clef, many bass notes would be almost unreadable in the forest of leger lines needed:

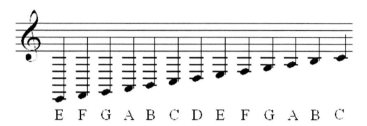

To overcome this problem, we simply redefine the stave for basses so that the basses' bottom notes are at the bottom of their stave:

To mark this, we use a different clef. The *bass clef* is said to be derived from an elaborate letter 'f' and the two dots highlight the second line down from the top of the stave as being F3.

The spaces in the bass clef are

A - C - E - G

which are traditionally rendered as "All Cows Eat Grass", which is hard to improve on.

The lines are

G - B - D - F - A

for which I can offer you "Grizzly Bears Drink Fizzy Ale".

The alto range is somewhat below the soprano but clearly higher than the bass. Altos used to have their own clef. But in modern notation they have to make do with the soprano clef and a bunch of leger lines. This is puzzling since the viola, with a range similar to the alto voice, still uses the old alto clef. But I suppose it does have the advantage that it makes it relatively easy for people to switch between soprano and alto parts without learning a new clef.

Tenors also used to have their own clef, but now also use the treble clef, albeit in a modified form. G is still G, but tenors sing the notes one octave lower than sopranos and altos. This is usually indicated by a small figure '8' under the clef or sometimes by two overlapping clefs. The most common forms are:

This practice – seeing one note and singing another – is called *transposition*. Tenors are said to transpose the soprano notes down an octave. The first note shown here looks like C4, middle C, but because the 8 sign indicates an octave transposition, it is actually C3.

Sometimes publishers print the tenor and bass lines on a single clef, which means that tenors get a raw deal, having to be able to read their transposing treble clef for when they get their own line, and also the bass clef for when they share one with the basses.

Stems

The stick attached to notes shorter than a semibreve is called its *stem*. Stems can point up or down, as illustrated above; this makes no difference to the note length. The normal rule is that stems point down for notes above the middle line and up for notes below.

When stems point up they go on the right of the note head, and when they point down they go on the left.

The tails, or flags, on quavers and other short notes however, always wave to the right.

The exception to the rule about stems going up on the lower part of the stave and down on the upper part, is when a single stave is used for two parts. Then the stems for the upper part <u>always</u> point up, and the stems for the lower part <u>always</u> point down. This can look confusing, as in the following example, showing a short extract for soprano and alto where the soprano line goes below the alto line in the second bar.

Key signatures

As we have seen, unless the piece of music is in C major or A minor, there will be "black key" notes. For example, if the piece is in G major, every F will be sharpened.

To avoid having to use lots of accidentals in the music composers write *key signatures* at the start of each line of music. The key signature lists all the sharps or flats needed to support the main key of the piece. It is therefore the surest way for the performer to tell what key the music is written in, (although a given key signature could relate to either a major key or to its relative minor).

For example, a key signature of two sharps could indicate either D major or B minor. Three flats could indicate E flat major or C minor, and so on.

There are various clues in the music itself which tell you whether you are in the relative major or minor, but perhaps the simplest is to look at the bottom note of the last chord of the piece; it will almost always, at least in pre-20th Century music, be the tonic note of the key.

This example of the (slightly modified) last two bars from one of the movements in Bach's *St Mathew Passion* illustrates this. The key signature of four flats could indicate either A flat major or F minor. The last note in the bass part is an A flat, suggesting that the piece is indeed in A flat major.

This example, simplified from the end of Gabrieli's *Lieto godea,* has the same key signature but is in F minor. Not only is the last bass note an F, but the D and E naturals in the second bar are characteristic of the F melodic minor scale.

For reference, the following table lists the first seven flat and sharp key signatures for both major and minor keys.

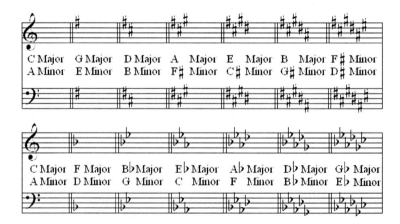

Note that key signatures always use the same pattern; you never see a key signature with, for example, the F sharp in a different octave.

Every major key uses the same set of intervals as every other major key, and every minor key uses the same set of intervals as every other minor key. Because of this, you will find that, as a singer, once you get comfortable with reproducing all the notes and intervals in major and minor scales you shouldn't have to worry too much about what key you're in. G flat major is just as easy a key to sing in as C major. The key signature does all the hard work for you of figuring out what notes need to be flattened or sharpened. Instrumentalists might find complicated key signatures difficult, but it's one thing singers don't have to worry too much about.

Accidentals

Any accidentals that occur during the piece have a much more limited shelf life than key signatures. An accidental lasts only until the next bar line. So if you come a cross a B with a flat sign next to it, making it a B flat, then you must sing any other Bs following it in the same bar as B flat too, unless cancelled by a natural; the accidental won't be repeated. But any Bs in subsequent bars are unaffected.

By the way, when you want to describe a note, you say its letter name first and then any accidental, for example "C sharp", "B flat" or "A Natural". But when you see the same notes written in a musical score the accidental always *precedes* the note. For example, this is F sharp:

Sharps always sharpen (raise the note one semitone) and flats always flatten (lower the note one semitone). But be careful about naturals. Naturals take the note back to its "white key" form. Sometimes this will mean lowering it a semitone, sometimes raising it. For example, if you are in the key of A major (three sharps) and you see a G natural, you must lower it a semitone from G sharp. But if you are in the key of G flat major and you see a G natural, you must raise it.

More on intervals and chords

I thought it would be useful at this point to go back and look at intervals again in the light of some of the above. In the following example, the first two intervals are seconds, the next two thirds, and so on. The first interval in each bar has its lower note on a line, the second in a space.

In this example I've used the common abbreviation for Octave, "8ve".

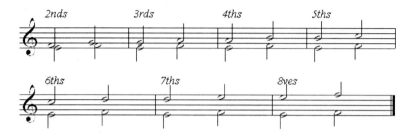

Incidentally, notice how with seconds, as in the first bar of the example, the convention is to move one of the notes slightly to the side to make it easier to read. This in no way alters the timing of the note.

The main thing I want you to notice, though is that with thirds, fifths and sevenths the notes are either both on a line or both on a space. With seconds, fourths, sixths and octaves, one note is always on a line and the other in a space.

This simple fact is extremely helpful in sight-reading, because it's one of the clues you can use to identify intervals at a glance.

The next example shows some triads in C Major. In part one we saw that triads are three-note chords made up from two notes a fifth apart with a third note in between. With triads in their simplest form, either all the notes are on lines, or all in spaces.

But you don't always see triads in this form. You can arrange the three notes in different ways. The basic position, as shown above, is called *root position* because it has the root of the chord at the bottom. If you put the original middle note on the bottom, this is called *first inversion* and if you put the original top note on the bottom, this is called *second inversion*.

Root position   1st inversion   2nd inversion

You can identify these three different positions by the characteristic intervals they include. Root position triads, as we have seen, have three evenly spaced notes. First inversion triads have a fourth between the top and middle notes. And second inversion triads have the fourth between the middle and bottom notes.

One common variation on this chord is to add a fourth note on the top, a third higher than the original top note. Because this new note forms the interval of a seventh with the root, this is known as a *seventh* chord.

We can see an example of these chords being used in practice in this slightly simplified and condensed extract from Haydn's *Creation*.

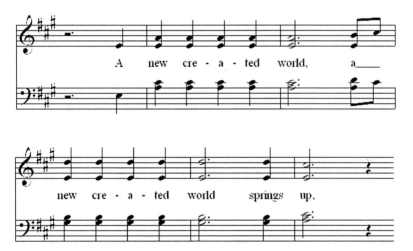

The first "new created world" is all sung on a root position triad in A major. The notes are A, C sharp and E, with the root note, A, repeated on top.

The second "new created world" is a seventh chord on the dominant, E. The notes are E, G sharp, B and D. It's a seventh because it's an interval of a seventh from the root of the chord, E to the top note, D.

The note in the bass is not the root E, however, but G sharp, because this chord is in first inversion.

This is an example of a very common type of seventh chord based around the dominant, and hence called a *dominant seventh*.

Another type of seventh chord is formed by piling three minor thirds on top of each other, for example A, C, E flat, G flat.

This chord is known as a *diminished seventh* and is an example of a chromatic chord since it uses non-diatonic notes; that is, notes outside the current key. Composers use diminished sevenths to add colour, and as a useful device as part of a modulation from one key to another. Beethoven was a great one for diminished sevenths. This example is from the "prisoners' chorus" in his opera *Fidelio*.

The diminished seventh in this example is made up from the notes F, A flat, B natural and D. This is shown on the left hand side below but it's easier to see why this is a seventh if you change the position of the chord as on the right hand side.

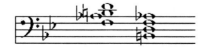

Cadences

A *cadence* is a chord pattern that ends a phrase, section or entire piece of music. There are different types of cadences for different occasions and we ought to take a quick look at the important ones.

A *perfect* cadence is one that moves from the dominant chord to the tonic chord. This is the most common cadence to find at the end of a piece.

An *imperfect* cadence is the opposite, ending on the dominant. You would not find this at the end of a piece, but it is very common in the middle.

A *plagal* cadence ends on the tonic like perfect cadence, but leads up to it from a chord on the subdominant. It's the "Amen" cadence you might hear at the end of a hymn.

An *interrupted* cadence sounds as if it's going to be a perfect cadence but slips off somewhere else, often to a chord on the sixth note of the scale, the submediant. Done right, this can give a startling effect since the submediant triad is a minor chord in a major key and a major one in a minor key.

There are some characteristic devices that you will often come across in cadences which I thought I'd mention here. Most pieces of music end with a perfect cadence. At one period it became common to end a minor key piece with a major triad by sharpening the mediant. This device is known as a *tierce de Picardy*, a 'Picardy third'. Nobody seems to know why.

The other device is rhythmical. In a piece written in triple time you may find a cadence in which the note lengths suddenly double, effectively halving the speed of the piece, and at the same time giving the music a syncopated feel. This device, common in 18th Century music, is known as a *hemiola*. The following example is taken from the end of the second movement of Vivaldi's *Gloria*.

This is equivalent to inserting a bar of 3/2 time, like this:

Phrasing

Almost everything we've talked about so far concerns what you might call the *mechanics* of music. Now it's time to talk about interpretation and performance.

A musical *phrase* is analogous to a phrase in spoken or written language; it's a group of notes that feel like they belong together as a unit.

In this nursery rhyme, there are clearly two phrases, as shown by the curved lines:

Twin-kle twin-kle litt-le star,   How I won-der what you are.

But sometime it's not quite so obvious. Let's look again at the extract from Haydn's Creation I used before when I was talking about triads and dominant sevenths. This time, though, we'll focus just on the melody.

How should this tune be phrased? It's partly a matter of interpretation. These two illustrations show two possible approaches, with the phrases marked out using curved lines (there are none in the original).

or

Phrases don't all have to be the same length. In fact, varying the phrase length is one of the ways composers can bring variety and interest into their music.

Unless the composer has been very precise about his intentions, it is up to the conductor or leader to make their own choices about phrasing. For singers, the text can often help. For example, the end of a phrase often coincides with a comma in the text. But this is only a rule of thumb – don't rely on it blindly.

Phrases are indicated through the use of curved lines called *slurs* which cover the whole phrase. This example is from Elgar's *Te deum laudamus* Op 34

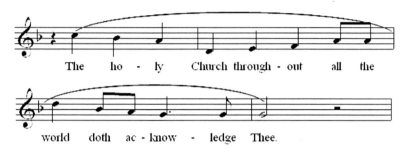

Ideally, you should plan to breathe at the end of each phrase, and not during it. Sometimes breath marks are marked in the score using either a comma or a V-shape. The difference is that a comma implies a short hesitation before the following note.

This example, slightly modified from *For all thy saints* by Alan Bullard, shows the use of the comma between phrases.

There are other, related but distinct, uses of the curved line notation. One is to denote two-note *slurs*. This example is from Elgar's *Give unto the Lord*:

When you see a slur like this, the composer is indicating that the notes should be sung with no break between them. It is also expected that the performer will stress the first note and 'float' the second one.

Another use of the curved line is really a special case of the slur, and has already been mentioned. When two notes at the same pitch are joined by a curved line, this is known as a *tie*. In this case the second note is not sounded afresh – the tie effectively creates a new note length made up of the combined lengths of both notes. Ties are used either when a note extends over a barline, as in this example from Mendelssohn's *Elijah*:

or to create a note length that couldn't be made any other way, as in this example from Britten's *Hymn to St. Cecilia*.

Finally, there is a special use confined to vocal music. Notes intended to be sung to a single syllable are joined under a curved line, as a way of emphasising the word-setting. This example is from Henry Purcell's *Celebrate this Festival*:

Articulation

The term *articulation* refers to the way the start of each note is handled.

The technique of playing or singing notes which are in an unbroken line is known as *legato* (from the Italian for "tied together") and is indicated either by phrase marks as described above or by the actual word *legato*.

The opposite of legato is *staccato*, meaning detached. This is indicated by a dot placed above or below the note, as in this example from Britten's *Ceremony of Carols*:

Staccato notes are generally reckoned to last about half the length of the note value shown. When the composer wants the notes as short and detached as possible they may use *staccatissimo* marks, which are like little arrowheads. This example is from Britten's *Rejoice in the Lamb*.

For the cym-bal rhimes are toll   soul   and the like___

Other articulation marks include *tenuto* where the note is slightly detached from its neighbours but held for at least its full value:

and *accent* which just implies a sudden strong attack to the note:

There are also various Italian terms which indicate a special way of articulating a note. Some common ones include:

fz or *sfz*   Sforzando - a sudden strong accent on an individual note

rf or *rfz*   Rinforzando - a sudden emphasis on a group of notes

fp   Fortepiano - loud then immediately soft

Pauses

Sometimes you are supposed to hold a note, or a rest, for an undefined amount longer than normal. This is indicated by a pause sign (a curve with a dot inside) written over or under a note or rest.

Almost invariably, you should also slow down slightly when approaching a pause.

Speed markings

At the beginning of each piece, you will see a number of important markings. Some of them we've already talked about: first comes the clef, then the key signature, which tells you which "black key" notes to use, and therefore which key the music is written in, and then the time signature which tells you how many beats there are in a bar.

You will likely also see some information about the basic speed, and possibly also the mood of the piece. This comes in the form of a word or phrase, which might be in Italian, but might also be in the composer's own language. Some common Italian speed indications are:

Largo	Slow, stately
Adagio	Slow
Andante	Medium to slow "walking" pace
Moderato	At a moderate speed
Allegretto	Fairly quick
Allegro	Quick
Vivace	Lively, quick
Presto	Fast

In the case of music dating from the eighteenth century or later there may also be a metronome mark. This consists of a note, an equals sign, and a number. For example:

$$\text{\musNote}=120$$

tells you to set your metronome to 120 clicks per minute, with each click representing a crotchet.

Dynamic markings

The term *dynamics* refers to how loud or soft the music should be.

Hairpins are wedge-shaped lines that indicate if the music needs to get louder or softer. This example, from Vaughan Williams' *Five mystical songs* illustrates both types of hairpins: for getting louder and softer.

high,   His   praise_____ may thith-er   fly: _____

A hairpin that starts off narrow at the left and gets wider indicates that you should get louder, and vice versa. Hairpins can cover a single note, or many.

There are also various Italian terms indicating dynamics. Here are some of the most common:

f	Forte	Strong, loud
ff	Fortissimo	Very loud
p	Piano	Soft, quiet
pp	Pianissimo	Very soft
mf	Mezzo forte	Medium loud
mp	Mezzo piano	Medium soft
Cresc.	Crescendo	Grow, get louder
Dim.	Diminuendo	Shrink, get softer
Decresc.	Decrescendo	Get softer

To indicate increasing degrees of quietness or loudness, composers sometimes pile on the *p* or *f* symbols: *ppp* is quieter than pianissimo and *fff* is louder than fortissimo.

Italian modifiers

There are a few Italian terms that crop up time and again in conjunction with the other terms we've discussed, and whose function is to modify the main term. Some of the main ones are listed here:

		Example
Meno	Less	Meno Allegro
Molto	Very, a lot	Allegro Molto
Non troppo	Not too much	Allegro non troppo
Più	More	Più Allegro
Poco	A little	Poco ritenuto
Poco a poco	Little by little	Poco a poco allargando
Subito	Suddenly	Subito Piano

Changes of tempo

Gradual or sudden changes in pulse are often marked in musical scores, using Italian words. Some examples are given here.

Rallentando (*Rall.*)   Gradually getting slower

Ritenuto (*Rit.*)   Held back

Accelerando (*Accel.*)   (ã-chel-er-an-dô) Gradually getting fast-er

Allargando   Broadening; a little slower and louder

A Tempo   (after Rit. etc.) Return to the speed immediately preceding the change

Rubato or *tempo rubato* from the Italian for 'robbed time' refers to a flexibility, or freedom, in the pulse. In performance, this means a hurrying or lingering in one part of a phrase, which should be compensated for later in the phrase.

Repeats

Music is full of repetition. Publishers take full advantage of this to reduce the amount of paper and ink they use. Choral singers must become adept at following the twists and turns of repeats. There are several notations to learn to do with repeats.

Let's start with the most basic. If you are supposed to repeat a section, it is marked with a special type of double bar line with added dots. Dots *after* the barline indicate the start of a repeated section, dots *before* it indicate the end. This example, from Britten's *Fishing song*, shows the sort of thing I mean. In this example you sing the top line of the words the first time through, and the lower line the second time, as shown by the verse numbers in front of each line.

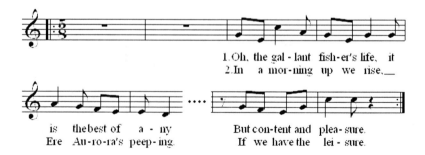

Another way to send you back to the beginning is the indication *D.C.* This stands for *Da Capo*, meaning literally *from the head*.

Having gone back to the beginning, you may not be meant to go all the way to the end again, but to stop at some mid-way point. This will be marked with the term *Fine*, meaning End.

So instead of just *D.C.* you may see *D.C al fine*. This indicates that you go back to the beginning and carry on until you get to the *Fine* sign. Then you stop.

A related expression to D.C. is *D.S.* This is short for *Dal Segno*, meaning *from the sign*. At some earlier point in the music there will be a symbol looking like this:

This is the "sign". So instead of going all the back to the beginning, you just go back to where you see the sign and carry on from there.

D.S. can also be teamed with "al Fine". D.S al fine means go back to the sign shown above and repeat, stopping when you come to the Fine sign.

First time and second time bars

Finally, we come to first time bars, after which this book is named, and their friends second time bars.

The basic idea is that you sing until you get to the repeat mark, passing under the first time bar line as you go. When you reach the repeat mark you go back to wherever it sends you.

Next time through, though, when you get to "first time bar" line you skip over the bar or bars underneath it and go straight to the section marked with the second time bar line.

In songs with several verses "first time bar" may actually be a bit of a misnomer. You may have to go round and round the repeated section several times. Eventually however, the "second time bar", or in this case the third, or fourth or fifth time bar will set you free.

The following example, from Britten's *The useful plough* shows an example of first and second time bars in action. The row of dots mark some music I've removed for the sake of clarity.

The words of the second verse begin "They rise with the morning lark". The "They" is immediately before the End Repeat sign which sends you back to the second bar of the extract. Notice also the small rhythm difference between the first and second verses, forced by the text and indicated by the extra note on "with the" with its tail pointing down:

Ornaments

Ornaments are musical flourishes that provide decoration to the melodic line. Most choral music is relatively ornament free because it's hard to pull off a tidy ornament in a group – it's a technique more suited to solo music. However you may see some so it's only fair to warn you.

Trill

One of the most common ornaments is the *trill* or *shake*. You perform it by rapidly alternating the written note with the one above. You may be asked to begin with the main note or with the one above; this is often a matter of interpretation and in case of uncertainty your conductor or choirmaster will tell you which. Trills are marked with the sign "tr", sometime followed by a squiggly line indicating the length of the trill.

The assumption is that the upper note will be diatonic, i.e. in the current key. However the composer may require a chromatic note to be used in which case this will be indicated with a small accidental.

Appoggiatura

The term *appoggiatura* comes from the Italian appoggiare meaning to lean on. An appoggiatura is written as a small note – called a *grace note* - preceding the main one. In performance, you usually place the grace note on the beat where the main note would have been. This obviously leaves less time for the main note. Normal practice is to divide the length equally between the two notes. The written appoggiatura is shown on the left, and suggested performance on the right:

Acciaccatura

The term *acciaccatura* (pronounced something like "at-chak-ka-t'your-er") means *crushed note* . It is written like an appoggiatura with a diagonal line through the tail and the idea is to sing it as quickly as possible before the main note. This example is from Britten's *Saint Nicholas*.

Abaft, aback, astern, abeam,

There are other types of ornaments but you are unlikely to come across them in choral music.

Glissando

A glissando (from the French glisser, to glide) is a musical effect made by sliding from one pitch to another. Glissandi (the plural of glissando) are written as either a straight diagonal or a squiggly line joining the two pitches, sometimes with the word "glissando" or "gliss." written next to the line.

This example, slightly modified from an arrangement of *Joshua fit the battle of Jericho* by Steve Barnett, illustrates two alternative notations:

Or

Other notation conventions

Swung quavers

Even though this book is largely about classical music I ought to mention the concept of swung quavers which you may need to know about if your choir does any jazz arrangements. In jazz, the convention is that pairs of quavers are written "straight" but are often required to be "swung". This means making the first one long and the second one short. Sing them pretty much as if they were triplets, with the first quaver taking up two-thirds of the time.

Lyrics

There are various conventions governing how the words you have to sing are written. Words of more than one syllable are usually broken up into individual syllables with hyphens, for example "Glo-ri-a". If a syllable extends over multiple notes, several hyphens in a row can be used. When the last, or only, syllable of a word has to be extended over multiple notes, this is shown with an unbroken line. This example, in German, is from Bach's *O Jesu Christ, meins Lebens Licht*.

Gast, nur_____ ein Gast, auf Er - den bin ich nur

Lyrics are usually placed immediately under the voice part, except when all the voice parts are written on two staves, a technique known as *short score*. In short score, in the case of a piece for mixed voices, sopranos and altos share the top stave, tenors and basses the second. In this case the lyrics will usually be between the two staves, so that tenors and basses have the text above their notes. If the word setting for each voice part is different, however, sometimes the text for sopranos and tenors will be above their respective staves and for altos and basses below. This is highly confusing, and I wish they wouldn't do it.

Rehearsal marks

In a long piece, the editor will often insert marks in the form of large letters or, sometimes, numbers, to act as a convenient place to start during rehearsals. When the conductor says things like "Seventeen before D", you need to get fast at finding D and counting back 17 bars - actually 17 bar *lines* would be more accurate - to see where you are going to start from.

Oh and while we're on the subject, I thought I'd mention the musician's slang "from the top". If your conductor says something like "Let's take it from the top", this means the beginning of the whole piece, rather than the top of the current page.

Which brings us to the end of this section. The next part of the book includes some thoughts on singing and spills the beans on some tricks of the choral singer's trade.

PART THREE: ABOUT SINGING

About singing

This section contains just a very few remarks on the fundamental business of getting the best out of your voice. I can't do more than scratch the surface of the topic here. If you would like to learn more then there are many books on vocal technique, but there is really no substitute to having proper lessons.

Using the voice well is about learning to control tone quality, resonance and breath. The source of the sound is the vocal folds in the larynx, at the top of the windpipe. This controls the tone. The sound is filtered through the vocal tract, the pipe that opens up inside the mouth and nasal cavity, which controls the resonance. Breath comes from the lungs, which delivers the power and helps to sustain the pitch.

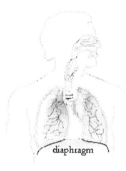

diaphragm

The vocal folds make the sound by vibrating so it's important that they can do this freely. Laughing, or pretending to laugh can help to open up the larynx, and many vocal exercises are designed to work on this area.

The diaphragm is a sheet of muscle which extends across the bottom of the ribcage. When you breathe in it contracts, creating the suction that draws air into the lungs. When it relaxes, air is expelled. When singers talk about support, they mean controlling the flow of air from the lungs and through the vocal folds. The diaphragm obviously plays a crucial role in singing, but unfortunately it's almost impossible to feel the diaphragm directly since it has few nerve endings. However, by keeping a good posture, and balance and by training the muscles of the stomach and surrounding structures, it is possible to strengthen the diaphragm to help support the breath.

Good posture in singing is a section in itself. Basically it comes down to standing up straight. Keep your shoulders back and down, legs straight but without locking the knees, feet slightly apart and chin about parallel to the floor.

Your mouth wants to open as freely as possible. Don't introduce tensions by singing with a wide mouth, try to open it north-south rather than east-west, even when singing an "ee" sound.

What you do immediately before you start singing is very important. Consciously breathe out by pulling your stomach in and then try to time things so that you take in a good deep breath early enough to fill your lungs but not so early that you end up having to hold your breath. Think about the first sound you are going to make and try to shape your mouth appropriately before you start.

Most choral singers sometimes worry that they may be singing out of tune. (In my experience it's the ones who never worry about it who are most likely to actually *be* out of tune). If you think you may be off pitch, stick a finger in one ear; it's much easier to hear yourself. If you find that you are a little off, it's much more likely that you are flat than sharp. Check your posture; the chances are that correcting your posture will correct the pitch.

Dealing with the text

Generally singers aim to *minimize* the time spent on consonants and *maximize* the time spent on vowel sounds. Thinking about the word "horse" for example, there are three sounds: the "h" at the beginning, the "or" vowel sound and the "s" sound at the end. Of the three, only the middle vowel can be "voiced" - in other words can carry a note. In singing, you would want to get onto it as quickly as possible and stay on it as long as possible.

Choral singers often find themselves singing the word "Gloria". As with "horse" it's a good idea to get the "gl" sound out of the way as quickly as possible and use the "o" sound in the middle to carry the note. In this case, it's more tricky to get round the double consonant of "gl" so this can mean beginning the sound of the word very slightly before the beat, so that the "gl" sound precedes the beat and the "o" sound comes exactly on it. The same applies to sounds like "pr" (as in "propter"), "sp" (as in "spiritu") and so on.

Similarly, at the end of a word, it's often important to make sure the final vowel sound continues as long as possible. For example, in this extract from the first movement of Mozart's *Requiem,* which is very slow, the composer almost certainly expects the final "s" sound to fall at the beginning of the second crotchet beat, and not at some point during the first crotchet.

lu - ce-at e - is.

Some more recent composers are very explicit about this sort of thing. For example in this extract from Vaughan Williams' *O be joyful in the Lord* , it is clear that he wants the word "song" to extend for a full bar, with the final "ng" falling at the beginning of the next bar or even just after the first beat.

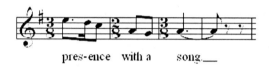

pres-ence with a   song.___

Tricks of the trade

Equipment

You don't need an awful lot of external equipment to sing in a choir: a bag to put your music in is useful; a bottle of water is a very good idea and a pencil to annotate your score with is vital. That's about it. It must be one of the cheapest hobbies there is!

One aid that many people find useful is the practice CD. Generally these are recorded using electronic sounds in place of the voice parts - so no lyrics - with one specific voice part picked out in a louder and more penetrating sound. There are several companies that produce a wide range of CDs covering at least the more frequently performed works in the choral repertoire. I have given contact details for one of these in the Appendix.

Finding your note

If I could tell you a foolproof way to find your note I would – but I'm afraid sometimes it's just hard. What you really want is perfect pitch. But if you had that you'd almost certainly know it already and wouldn't be reading this section.

Perfect pitch, better called *absolute pitch*, is simply the ability to recognise or reproduce a note without reference to other notes. A person with absolute pitch will recognise, say, an A, as an A regardless of the context. To him or her an A couldn't be anything else because it has a quality of "A-ness" about it that makes it impossible to confuse with another note in the same way that a person with good colour vision can recognise the colour "red" without needing to compare it with anything else. It is thought that there is a strong genetic component in this ability, although it seems as if it can to some extent be taught in infancy. If you're an adult and you don't have it I'm afraid that chances are you're not going to get it.

What you can do, though, is improve your sense of relative pitch. You can invent all sorts of games and exercises to help with this: play a note on the piano and sing another. Start off with relatively simple intervals like octaves and seconds, and then challenge yourself.

What you're always hoping for, of course, is to hear your note played or sung just before you are expected to sing it. Often you'll be lucky. Look in the score to see if your note is in one of the other parts, even if it's an octave higher or lower. If not, perhaps it's there in the accompaniment.

If you can't find your actual note, perhaps you can find another note you can use as a springboard, where you can find the correct interval. Most composers were, and are, aware of the needs of the amateur singer and have built in little aids into the music – if you can spot them!

It's tempting, but a bad long term strategy to rely too heavily on the person standing next to you for your note. It damages the rhythmic precision of the choir by creating an in-built delay. It also deprives you of the pleasure and feeling of achievement you get when you do it yourself. And it means you get heart-failure when you turn up to rehearsal one week and find that they're away! Make it your mission and your responsibility to become self-reliant.

Coping with languages

Not all choral music is in English. In fact at times it seems like not much of it is. Much sacred music is, inevitably, in Latin. But you should never shy away from singing music in other languages too. Your conductor will help to make sure you pronounce the words intelligently, and you may need to be prepared to move your mouth in very different ways to achieve some foreign sounds.

Annotating your score

Most musicians find their own way of annotating their copies of the score with additional instructions or warnings. A few common ones are worth mentioning as many people find them useful.

Where it isn't obvious, you can remind yourself where you are supposed breathe by drawing in a comma or a V-shape.

It's very easy to miss important but small directions like Rit. with potentially disastrous results. Many musicians draw squiggly horizontal lines across the bar or bars where the music should slow down to help remind them.

If your voice part has an entry in an unexpected place, for example immediately after a page turn, many people draw a picture of a pair of glasses immediately before as a warning.

Repeat marks are also easy to miss, and sometimes it can be hard to find quickly the beginning of the repeat. Many musicians draw chevron shapes at the start and end to help them stand out.

Lastly, in scores with many voice parts, or frequent changes in the number of staves on a page, it's well worth going through the score between rehearsals marking your own part with arrows or asterisks. It goes without saying that you should always annotate in pencil, rather than pen.

Choral voice parts and ranges

Sopranos are expected to be able to reach from just below C4 to G5 or A5. If you haven't got those top notes you can still be a soprano, but you will need to work on extending your range. Boy sopranos are also called trebles and have a similar range to adult sopranos.

The alto range is about a fifth lower than the soprano range, so from about F3 to C5 or D5 above it.

Tenors are about a fourth lower than altos, so about an octave below sopranos. Their range goes from somewhere around C3 to G4 or A4. Some female voices are able to span this range and lady tenors are by no means unknown. Since male tenors are always in short supply, most choirs welcome lady tenors with open arms (I'm speaking metaphorically here).

Basses are about a fifth lower than tenors, so about an octave below altos. Their range goes from about E2 or F2 to around C4 or D4.

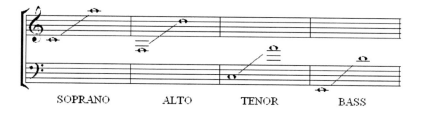

SOPRANO   ALTO   TENOR   BASS

Conductors

Whether you call them "choral director", "choirmaster" or "conductor", why do we need these people? It's a question that is often asked, although admittedly not generally when the conductor is there.

I think the conductor performs two main functions. The first is to be the interpreter of the music. The ultimate performance should be a reflection of the conductor's musical "vision" of the piece. This covers everything from tempo and dynamics to more subtle aspects of breathing, phrasing and so on. In this sense the choir is almost literally the conductor's "instrument". This includes prosaic, but vital, things like making sure everyone starts and stops at the same time.

Since the choral instrument is made of human beings, the second main purpose of the conductor is a more human one. It is to inspire; to focus and direct the energy of every choir member to enhance the group activity of singing. This might sound rather pretentious, but truthfully I don't know how else to put it. I think if you've sung in a choir you will know what I'm talking about; that magic thing that happens in choirs (sometimes) when everything just clicks and the choral sound takes on a life and energy of its own which is somehow more than the sum of the individuals in the group. Ultimately that's what the conductor is for – to take you to "Choral Nirvana".

Beat patterns and gestures

Conductors make a lot of strange movements, and choral conductors possibly even more so. If you sing with enough of them you'll see just about every hand gesture known to man. Some of them will be more helpful than others. I can't hope in this short section to give you an encyclopaedic account of every gesture you're likely to see, but I will try to demystify the bizarre hand-dancing you put up with at each rehearsal.

Many conductors think of a point in space a few inches in front of their body, a little lower than their chest, as representing the point of the beat. In some "textbook" conducting styles the conductor's beating hand returns to this point at exactly the start of each beat, although in others, the beat happens at different places in space.

The first beat of every bar is called a "downbeat" because the conductor's arm should, in theory, make some kind of a downward movement at this point. Depending on the style of music the beat itself will usually be indicated by a little flick of the fingers, hand or wrist.

It follows then that the last beat of each bar must be an "upbeat" – you have to go up before you can come down. In theory it should start away from the conductor's body and sweep inwards and upwards. So if your conductor is right-handed, you will see the upbeat coming from his right – your left.

The upbeat at the start of a piece or section should tell you all you need to know about the speed and mood of what you're about to sing, so watch it like a hawk.

There are textbook beat patterns for each time signature. All books for conductors show this from the conductor's perspective, but since you are standing facing the conductor, I have shown some examples from your perspective, which of course is the **mirror-image**. Here are diagrams for 2, 3 and 4 beats in a bar. To follow these, start at the top; the dots represent the actual beats

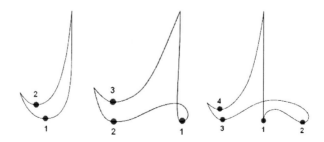

All conductors develop, over time, a wide range of gestures based on what they find works best for them. Some wave their arms like windmills, others make tiny movements. Most use an open hand position and some have very expressive fingers. To indicate a loud ending for the last note of a piece many conductors make an expansive sideways gesture of the arms. To help the choir end together on a soft ending, many bring their fingers gently together in front of them much in the manner of a person pulling a hair out of their soup.

Often conductors will subdivide a beat, making a smaller flick on each half-beat. This is very common in a slow 4/4 time, when a conductor will often let you know they are going to beat "in 8".

By convention most choral conductors do not use a baton, the white stick used by most orchestral conductors, unless conducting a choir and orchestra together.

Positions

There is no one universally accepted way of arranging the voice parts in a choir. It depends on a lot of factors, such as the size and shape of the space available, the type of music, and the conductor's particular ideas. Normally sopranos stand on the conductor's left, but that's about it as far as conventions go.

Sometimes the lower voices stand behind the higher voices, sometimes alongside them. When singing with an orchestra, especially in music of the Classical period, sometimes the voice parts are arranged so that they are near the string section that most closely follows their part: sopranos with first violins, altos with second violins, tenors with violas and basses with cellos.

Sometimes conductors will arrange the choir so that the voice parts are mixed up together. This obviously requires a higher degree of self-sufficiency on the part of each singer, but it works very well with some types of music and some choirs.

Types of choir

There are many different types of choir, and it's important to join one in which you feel comfortable, and which is going to give you the opportunity to sing the type of music you enjoy.

Mixed voice choirs usually include Soprano, Alto, Tenor and Bass parts, with each voice part sometimes divided into first and second. Sometimes there is a separate baritone section, and sometimes the men's voices are combined into one part. Men's and women's choirs make use of exclusively low or high voices

Many or most churches run choirs if they can, to support the music during services, and these choirs often give occasional additional concerts.

Some choirs specialise in particular types of music such as oratorio, jazz or stage shows.

England in particular is also rich in choral societies; community choirs with a wide remit to sing virtually any type of music they enjoy. It's astonishing how many choirs there are around - almost wherever you live there's sure to be one near.

Auditions

Many choirs are more than happy to accept all comers, but some choirs demand that you go through an audition process before they let you in. Even if you pass the audition, you may have to go through a probation period before you can consider your place assured.

Even if you are not an experienced singer, don't let the audition process put you off from applying – it isn't necessarily a sign of unfriendliness and you never know, you may be just the person they are looking for.

The only advice I can give you about the audition itself is try to relax, and try not to take it personally if you don't get in. Most choirs aren't looking for the next Pavarotti, but for a voice that they think will blend with the existing choir sound, so whatever you are asked to sing, just stand up straight, sing in your normal voice and don't try to force some kind of unnatural sound out.

And that's the end of this short section. The final part of the book contains some general musical knowledge which I think is of relevance and interest to choir singers.

PART FOUR: REPERTOIRE

Choral singers are blessed with a vast range of repertoire ranging over several centuries and many countries. The following is a very brief scamper through the territory to give you a feeling for what's out there.

Musical Periods

First, a lightning tour through the major periods of Western musical history to help you orientate yourself.

Western musical history is commonly divided into several periods according to the musical styles and aesthetic movements of the time. These can be summarised as: Mediaeval; Renaissance; Baroque; Classical; Romantic; and everything that comes after Romantic.

Because music in the middle ages was an almost exclusively aural tradition, we have relatively few examples of vocal music from this period apart from monastic chants and some secular songs.

The monastic tradition of chants, itself strongly influenced by traditional Jewish psalm singing, was of great importance because out of it grew the basis of harmony and counterpoint. The music itself survives, not least in a living tradition of plainsong in the Roman Catholic Church and in the chorale tunes which the Lutheran church borrowed from plainsong. By the 12th century the various chanting traditions had been standardised as *Gregorian chant*, which dates back as far as the 9th century.

Perhaps the best known examples in Britain of secular mediaeval music are the famous round *Summer is a-cumin in* written in about 1250 and the early 15th century *Agincourt Song* written, it is assumed, soon after the battle which took place in 1415. One important musical tradition at this time was associated with troubadours, who were composers and performers. This tradition, closely associated with the ideals of chivalry and courtly love originated in France in the 11th century.

The most eminent English composer of the late mediaeval period was John Dunstable who died in 1453. Most of his surviving works are Masses, or Mass movements, and a few secular songs. John Taverner, born around 1490, is remembered primarily for some fine Mass settings including the "Western Wind" Mass probably written in the 1540's.

In general there isn't an awful lot of secular English music from the late Middle Ages left. Songs like *Greensleeves* and *Pastime with good Company*, said to have been written by Henry VIII (who died in 1547) give just a flavour of what secular music was like at this time.

The Renaissance (from an old French word meaning rebirth) is a term used to refer to a cultural movement that flourished from about the late 15th and into the 16th and 17th centuries. It was a time of enormous artistic and scientific change and music flourished along with the other arts. Famous composers from this period include Giovanni da Palestrina, Claudio Monteverdi, Guillaume Dufay, William Byrd and Henry Purcell. The Italian and English Madrigalists fall in this period too: Orlando Gibbons, Thomas Morley and others.

The term Baroque is usually used to refer to a period from about the end of the 16th Century to the middle of the 18th. In art or architecture the term "Baroque" is often associated with complicated decorative flourishes and the baroque period in music has some of that too. Baroque music often contains complicated part-writing where the voices interweave to create a seamless texture. The period also saw the invention of new musical forms such as Oratorio. Baroque composers you are likely to come across include J.S. Bach, George Frederic Handel and Antonio Vivaldi.

The Classical period, roughly the late 18th and early 19th centuries, was a time of consolidation in music. Musical development in this period centred on Austria and in particular Vienna. Part-writing tended to get simpler, and harmony more daring. Some religious choral music of the period harks back to the style of earlier periods but used in a somewhat self-conscious manner. Composers of choral music from the Classical period include Joseph Haydn and Wolfgang Amadeus Mozart. These two figures are so huge that they tend to blot out everything else but of course there were other good composers around, including Johann Hummel, and the Italian-born Antonio Salieri.

The Romantic period, roughly the latter part of the 19th century, corresponds with romantic periods in literature and other arts. This music tends to be harmonically more intricate and daring than before, and more overtly emotional. Major Romantic composers of choral music include Franz Schubert, Felix Mendelssohn, Johannes Brahms, Giuseppe Verdi and Gabriel Fauré.

The romantic period ended somewhere around the turn of the twentieth century but since then the proliferation of musical styles and aesthetics has been so bewildering that even now, over a hundred years later, it's not clear what term, if anything, could be used to cover it all.

Choral music, perhaps because it is still dominated by amateur music-makers, remains relatively accessible compared with much contemporary orchestral and instrumental music. People have taken many pieces of 20th and 21st century and contemporary choral music to their hearts in a way that hasn't really happened to the same extent with other types of classical music. From British composers alone I'm thinking particularly of people like Benjamin Britten, Michael Tippett, Ralph Vaughan Williams, John Rutter, Bob Chilcott and Karl Jenkins to name but a few.

Beyond the traditional European music I learned about at music college in the seventies, choirs today also have unparalleled access to many different vibrant music traditions from around the World, including Africa and South America. Add to that more popular styles, including gospel, jazz, Broadway, pop song arrangements and so on, and the contemporary choir today need never be short of exciting new material.

Musical texture

I really hate to bother you with more technical terms, but there are some particularly useful words you may come across which describe different types of musical texture, or style: polyphony, counterpoint, and homophony.

Polyphony and Counterpoint

The terms polyphony and counterpoint both refer to a musical texture in which there are two or more musical lines that move independently of one another. Historically this technique originally developed between the 10th and 13th centuries.

The word polyphony (adjective *polyphonic*) comes from the Greek *polyphonia* meaning 'many sounds', and is normally only used when talking about music of the Renaissance period.

Baroque music often uses a very similar technique of independent parts but this is normally referred to as *counterpoint* (adjective *contrapuntal*). This term comes from the Latin *punctus contra punctus* meaning 'note against note'.

Homophony

Homophony describes music in which one part is melodic and the other parts mainly chordal, or else in which there is very little rhythmic independence between the parts. Many part songs (see below) use this style and are therefore referred to as being *homophonic*.

In practice, few pieces are entirely polyphonic/contrapuntal or entirely homophonic, but blend the two together, with one or other style coming to the fore. Here are some examples of each type of texture taken from two pieces of choral music written 300 years apart.

The polyphonic example is from *Sicut cervus* by the 16th century Italian Renaissance composer Palestrina

And this homophonic piece is from *Salve Regina* by the 19th century French Romantic composer Poulenc.

Classical musical forms

A large proportion of the music sung by most choirs is sacred, that is either written for use as part of a religious service, or based on a religious text or theme. As a major consumer of choral music over many centuries, the Christian Church is responsible for commissioning or sponsoring many of the great choral works of the past and present.

Mass and Requiem

A musical Mass is a setting of the fixed portions of the liturgy for Holy Communion. Most early Mass settings were intended for use during actual services but many of the more recent works were designed primarily or entirely for concert use.

Generally Masses include five or six movements, named after the opening word or words of each section: Kyrie, Gloria, Credo, Sanctus, Benedictus, Agnus Dei. Often the Sanctus and Benedictus are combined into one movement.

The earliest Mass settings to survive date back to the 14th Century, including the *Notre Dame Mass* by Guillaume de Machaut. There have been many fine settings of the Mass, some incorporating additional text of the composer's choosing. Particularly well-known works include the *Mass in B Minor* by J.S. Bach, the *Mass in C Minor* by Mozart (1782), The so-called *"Nelson" Mass* (1798) and *Mass in Time of War* (1796) by Haydn, the *Missa Solemnis* (1820) by Beethoven and the *Petite Messe Solenelle* (1864) by Rossini

Requiem Masses are specifically intended as prayers for the departed, and may be written to be used at services preceding a burial, or for occasions of more general remembrance. Famous musical Requiems include settings by Mozart (1791), Gabriel Fauré (1877) and Guiseppi Verdi (1873). The Requiem form includes additional movements not found in the normal Mass.

Passion

Passion settings reflect the Gospel story of the Crucifixion and so are particularly associated with Easter. By far the best know musical Passion settings are J.S. Bach's *St. John Passion* (1724) and *St. Matthew Passion* (1727). Astonishingly, the St. Matthew Passion, one of the most famous works in the entire canon was never heard outside of Leipzig until it was performed, in abbreviated form, by Felix Mendelssohn in Berlin in 1829, over a century after it was written.

Oratorio

Oratorios are large musical compositions for orchestra, choir and soloists. The subject matter may be almost anything, religious or otherwise, and the effect is somewhat like an unstaged opera, although the plot, if any, tends to be minimal. Famous oratorios include Handel's *Messiah* (1741) and *Israel in Egypt* (1738), Haydn's *Creation* (1794) and *The Seasons* (1800), Mendelssohn's *Elijah* (1846) and Berlioz' *L'enfance du Christ* (1854).

Cantata

Cantata is a vague term that literally means music that is sung. One of the few generalisations you can make about the form is that a cantata usually has instrumental music and more than one movement. Famous examples include nearly 200 works by J.S. Bach.

Motet

Another vague term, motet means a piece of sung music in several parts. Most motets date back to Renaissance times and there are many early examples by Byrd, Orlando di Lasso, Giovanni da Palestrina, Thomas Tallis, and others. J.S. Bach wrote seven motets that survive, including the famous *Singet dem Herrn ein neues Lied* (1726).

Magnificat

A Magnificat, or Song of Mary, is a biblical hymn (canticle) based on the story of the Annunciation and subsequent visit of Mary to her relative Elizabeth, the mother-to-be of John the Baptist. The most famous Magnificat is probably the setting by J.S. Bach (who else?) written in 1733. Its is often set together by Anglican composers with the Nunc Dimittis, or Canticle of Simeon: "Lord, now lettest Thou Thy servant depart in peace".

Te Deum Laudamus

Te Deum Laudamus, which in Latin means 'We praise Thee, O God', is a hymn of rejoicing in both the Roman Catholic and Anglican Churches. The text dates back at least to the 4th Century and is used as part of morning prayers. There are many settings of the hymn, including those by Henry Purcell (1694), George Frederic Handel (1713 and 1743), Hector Berlioz (1855) and others.

Stabat Mater

Stabat Mater dolorosa, which in Latin means 'Sorrowfully His mother stood' is part of the Roman Catholic liturgy, and associated with Passion Week. The poem is of unknown origin and has been set by many composers including Giovanni da Palestrina, Joseph Haydn (1767), Schubert (1815), Gioachino Rossini (1832) and C.V. Stanford (1907).

Anthem

Anthems are specifically Anglican, and can be settings of any religious text, originally in English but more recently potentially also in Latin. There are many early examples by Purcell (written for the Chapel Royal), Byrd and Tallis, and more recent ones by Edward Elgar, Charles Villiers Stanford and others.

Spiritual and Gospel music

Spirituals, or "negro spirituals" were folk songs of a religious nature created by American slaves to provide comfort, or to express a thinly disguised longing for freedom. Famous examples include *Swing Low, Sweet Chariot* and *Steal Away to Jesus*. Many composers have made arrangements of spirituals, one of the most famous uses being the five spirituals which Michael Tippet uses as punctuation in his oratorio *A Child of Our Time*.

Gospel music is a Twentieth Century innovation that fuses spirituals with Christian hymns. Unlike spirituals, which are usually sung unaccompanied, gospel music is often accompanied by a drum kit and often other instruments too.

Madrigal

The madrigal form dates back to the Renaissance and early Baroque eras. Madrigals are short, polyphonic songs, often with text written by the composer on a fanciful pastoral theme. Starting in Italy in the 1520s, the fashion spread to England in the late 1580s. Although it lasted a relatively short time, this period saw a great flowering of musical invention in those countries. Famous English madrigalists include William Byrd, Orlando Gibbons, Thomas Morley, John Dowland, Thomas Weelkes and John Wilbye. Italian madrigalists included Claudio Monteverdi, Orlando di Lasso, Carlo Gesualdo, and Luca Marenzio.

Part song

The term part song can be applied to almost any short work for multiple voices, but part songs are usually homophonic rather than contrapuntal in nature, with the top part carrying the melody and lower parts the harmony. There are part songs by Schubert, Schumann and Mendelssohn, but the genre is probably most closely associated with England where the 19th Century growth in choral societies created a huge demand. Victorian and Edwardian composers like Edward Elgar, Hubert Parry, Charles Villiers Stanford, Arthur Sullivan and many others contributed part songs. One of the best known is possibly Stanford's *The Blue Bird*.

Folk song arrangement

In the first part of the Twentieth Century a small group of composers and musicians, including Cecil Sharp, Percy Grainger, Gustav Holst and Ralph Vaughan Williams, began travelling around the English countryside collecting folks songs. This music became extremely influential in the development of a particularly English style of composition, and many composers have created arrangements of the songs collected during this period. Apart from the composers mentioned, Peter Warlock, E.J. Moeran and more recently John Rutter, David Willcocks and many others have contributed to this repertoire.

Popular music and jazz

Many choral arrangements are available of different kinds of popular music, from the 1920s to the present day, and of music from films and stage shows.

Jazz, being an improvised musical language, doesn't directly lend itself easily to choral singing, but there is a wealth of written music which uses a jazz-inspired idiom available. A recent example is Bob Chilcott's *Little Jazz Mass*.

World music

World music is a catch-all term for traditional music, or music based on traditional roots from anywhere in the World. It effectively means any music other than Western classical ("Art") music, or Western popular music. Many people dislike the term as being too vague and driven largely by marketing, but I don't know a better one.

Today's choirs are lucky enough to have a huge range of music to choose from, including music based on, or inspired by, the traditional music of Eastern Europe, the Middle East, Africa and South America.

* * * * *

That brings us to the end of this section, and the end of this book. I hope you have found it useful and interesting and I also hope the information in this book will encourage you to learn more about music theory and notation, music history and the art of choral singing generally.

Timeline of composers mentioned

To help you get a sense of who came when, this table lists, in chronological order, all the composers who happen to be mentioned in the book, along with their dates and nationality.

14th Century

Machaut, Guillaume de	c.1300-1377	French
Dunstable, John	c.1390-1453	English
Dufay, Guillaume	c.1397-1474	Franco-Flemish

15th Century

Taverner, John	c.1490-1545	English

16th Century

Tallis, Thomas	c.1505-1585	English
Palestrina, Giovanni da	c.1525-1594	Italian
Lasso, Orlando di	c.1532-1594	Franco-Flemish
Byrd, William	c.1534-1623	English
Marenzio, Luca	c.1553-1599	Italian
Gabrieli, Giovanni	c.1555-1612	Italian
Morley, Thomas	1557-1602	English
Gesualdo, Carlo	c.1560-1613	Italian
Dowland, John	1563-1626	English
Monteverdi, Claudio	1567-1643	Italian
Wilbye, John	1574-1638	English
Weelkes, Thomas	1576-1623	English
Gibbons, Orlando	1583-1625	English

17th Century

Purcell, Henry	1659-1695	English
Vivaldi, Antonio	1678-1741	Italian
Bach, Johann Sebastian	1685-1750	German
Handel, George Frederic	1685-1759	German

18th Century

Haydn, Joseph	1732-1809	Austrian
Salieri, Antonio	1750-1825	Italian
Mozart, Wolfgang Amadeus	1756-1791	Austrian
Beethoven, Ludwig van	1770-1827	German
Hummel, Johann Nepomuk	1778-1837	Austrian
Rossini, Gioachino	1792-1868	Italian
Schubert, Franz	1797-1828	Austrian

19th Century

Berlioz, Hector	1803-1869	French
Mendelssohn, Felix	1809-1847	German
Verdi, Giuseppe	1813-1901	Italian
Brahms, Johannes	1833-1897	German
Sullivan, Arthur	1842-1900	English
Fauré, Gabriel	1845-1924	French
Parry, Hubert	1848-1918	English
Stanford, Charles Villiers	1852-1924	Irish
Elgar, Edward	1857-1934	English
Vaughan Williams, Ralph	1872-1958	English
Holst, Gustav	1874-1934	English
Grainger, Percy Aldridge	1882-1961	Australian
Warlock, Peter	1894-1930	Anglo-Welsh
Moeran, Ernest John	1894-1950	English
Poulenc, Francis	1899-1963	French

20th Century

Tippett, Michael	1905-1998	English
Britten, Benjamin	1913-1976	English
Willcocks, David	b.1919	English
Jenkins, Karl	b.1944	Welsh
Rutter, John	b.1945	English
Chilcott, Bob	b.1955	English

Appendix - Useful contacts and links

This is a partial, personal and entirely subjective list of some resources that you might find useful.

Rehearsal CDs

There are several companies that offer rehearsal tapes and CDs which help choral singers learn their parts. If you find these useful, and many people do, then the Choraline series from Music Dynamics Ltd are popular and well made. Their web address is musicdynamics.co.uk.

Making Music

Make sure the people who run your choir know about Making Music, The National Federation of Music Societies. This is open to everyone involved in voluntary music and offers many different services to choirs. Their web address is www.makingmusic.org.uk.

Gerontius

This is just a really useful website, full of choral music resources. Its address is www.gerontius.net

The Really Big Chorus

This is the organisation that runs the "Concerts From Scratch" events in the Royal Albert Hall in London and elsewhere, where thousands of singers come together to rehearse and then perform a major work. They are great fun, and if you feel unsure of the music there's definitely safety in numbers. Their web address is www.trbc.co.uk.

Choral Society

Choral Society is a website resource for "choral singers who are passionate about their singing". Its address is www.choralsociety.info

Free Music

You'll be amazed at how much sheet music you can download, quite legitimately, from the internet. A good place to start is the Choral Public Domain Library at www.cpdl.org.

Leith Hill Musical Festival

I have no real excuse for mentioning this here except that I think it's just wonderful. This choral festival takes place over three days every Spring in Dorking, in Surrey and has been going for over 100 years. It was conducted for many years by its founder conductor the composer Ralph Vaughan Williams. Its website is www.lhmf.co.uk.

Three Choirs Festival

This international choral and orchestral festival takes place in rotation in Gloucester, Hereford and Worcester. Its web address is www.3choirs.org.

Index

T

Printed in the United Kingdom
by Lightning Source UK Ltd.
130897UK00001B/272/P